THE
ESSENTIAL
UN

D1715135

The Essential UN

Published by the United Nations
New York, New York 10017, United States of America

All queries on rights and licenses,
including subsidiary rights, should be addressed to:

United Nations Publications
300 East 42nd Street
New York, New York 10017
United States of America

E-mail: publications@un.org; website: http://shop.un.org

Requests to reproduce excerpts should be addressed to:
permissions@un.org

ISBN: 9789211013726
eISBN: 9789213626993(PDF)
ePUB: 9789213582121

United Nations Publication Sales No. 17.I.10

Design and layout
Outreach Division
Department of Public Information
United Nations, New York

FIGHT FEAR WITH FAITH

"For God has not given us a spirit of fear, but of power and of love and of a sound mind." 2 Timothy 1:7

"Be anxious for nothing, but in everything by prayer and supplication, with thanksgiving, let your requests be made known to God; and the peace of God, which surpasses all understanding, will guard your hearts and minds through Christ Jesus." Philippians 4:6-7

"Do not be anxious about your life, what you will eat, nor about your body, what you will put on." Luke 12:22

"Fear not, for I am with you." Isaiah 41:10

"Fear not, little flock!" Luke 12:32

CHRISTIANS IN DEFENSE OF ISRAEL
PO BOX 540209
ORLANDO, FL 32854
(407) 875-1948   CIDISRAEL.ORG
©2020

9 POINTS OF RESOLVE

For Overcoming Fear

1 **WE WILL** not fear because we serve the Creator and our Redeemer. "Fear not, little flock."

2 **WE WILL** not add to the panic.

3 **WE WILL** speak peace to all we encounter.

4 **WE WILL** minister to the world the Light of the world.

5 **WE WILL** be the church that Jesus called us to be and run to, not from, danger to save souls.

6 **WE WILL** remember that the Gates of Hell shall not prevail against the church.

7 **WE WILL** pray that the COVID-19 virus is crushed.

8 **WE WILL** pray for wisdom for our elected leaders.

9 **WE WILL** spend more time in the Word of God than we spend chasing media stories.

TABLE OF CONTENTS

Chapter 1

AN INTRODUCTION
TO THE UNITED NATIONS

QUICK FACTS ABOUT THE UNITED NATIONS

- The United Nations was initially conceived as a wartime alliance on 1 January 1942, and established as an international organization on 24 October 1945. To commemorate the creation of the United Nations, the world celebrates **United Nations Day** each year on 24 October.

- The United Nations has **four purposes**: (1) to maintain international peace and security; (2) to develop friendly relations among nations; (3) to cooperate in solving international problems and promoting respect for human rights; and (4) to be a centre for harmonizing the actions of nations. More than 30 affiliated organizations cooperate in this effort. They are known together as the **United Nations system**, and all have their own specific areas of work.

- The United Nations is **not a world government**. However, it does provide the means to help resolve international conflicts and formulate policies on matters affecting all of us. The United Nations is a forum where all countries meet to discuss, elaborate and extend international law in areas such as human rights, international trade, the sea, and the fight against terrorism.

- At the United Nations, all the Member States—large and small, rich and poor, with differing political views and social systems—have a voice and a vote in making decisions in the **General Assembly**.

- The United Nations System works to promote respect for human rights, reduce poverty, fight disease and protect the environment. The United Nations leads **international campaigns** against drug trafficking and terrorism, as well as to eliminate violence against women and to protect natural ecosystems.

- The United Nations and its agencies undertake a myriad of **projects throughout the world**, including assisting refugees; fighting AIDS and malaria; expanding food production; protecting labour; supporting education for all, and providing help after natural disasters and armed conflicts.

The idea of a peaceful world community

Although the United Nations came into being during the Second World War (1939–1945), the ideal of a community of nations living in peace was conceived much earlier. In 1795, the German philosopher Immanuel Kant developed the idea of perpetual peace, a doctrine based on what we now call the rule of law. He advocated that nations establish a peaceful world community, not through a global government, but with each country becoming a free State respectful of its citizens and foreign visitors, thus promoting a peaceful society worldwide.

With this idea, Kant not only influenced philosophical and political thinking, he also sparked the development of international law and the creation of institutions such as the Inter-Parliamentary Union (established in 1889, a forerunner to the League of Nations and, today, a Permanent Observer at the United Nations). His influence is likewise clearly visible in the "Fourteen Points" speech given by American President Woodrow Wilson to the United States Congress on 8 January 1918, which included the first mention of the League of Nations.

The League of Nations

The League of Nations was set up in 1919, following the First World War. It was officially established when 44 countries signed the Covenant of the League of Nations, the first part of the Treaty of Versailles.

The main objective of the League of Nations was to keep world peace by promoting disarmament, preventing war through collective security, settling disputes between countries through negotiation and diplomacy and improving global welfare.

However, the League had certain fundamental weaknesses. If States involved in a dispute chose to ignore the League's decisions, the League could introduce economic sanctions; since it did not have a military force, it had no way of enforcing those decisions.

In addition, not all countries were members of the League of Nations. The United States, for example, was never a member, despite President Wilson's efforts and involvement in the League's creation. Other States that had joined later quit, and the League often failed to take action when necessary.

Despite these weaknesses, the League of Nations was able to resolve some disputes and stop some local wars. It successfully intervened in the dispute between Sweden and Finland over the Aaland Islands (1921) and stopped Greece's invasion of Bulgaria (1925). However, it was ineffective in preventing or stopping powerful nations from fighting. When Italy invaded Abyssinia (Ethiopia) in 1935, the League condemned the act of aggression and imposed sanctions, but the sanctions had no impact. Moreover, the League was powerless in the face of events leading up to the Second World War.

Though it did not succeed, the League of Nations initiated the dream of a universal organization. Its successor was the United Nations, which inherited the assets and property of the dissolved League, worth approximately $22 million in 1946, including the Palais des Nations in Geneva (Switzerland) and the League's archives.

Creation of the United Nations

The idea of the United Nations was born during the Second World War. Allied world leaders who had collaborated to end the war felt a strong need for a mechanism that would help bring peace and stop future wars. They realized that this was possible only if all nations worked together through a global organization. The United Nations was to be that organization.

Declaration of St. James's Palace

In June 1941, London was the home of nine exiled governments. The resilient British capital had already endured months of war, and in the bomb-marked city, air-raid sirens wailed all too frequently. Practically all of Europe had fallen to the Axis Powers, and ships on the Atlantic carrying vital supplies sank with grim regularity. But in London itself, and among the Allied governments and peoples, faith in the ultimate victory remained unshaken.

On 12 June 1941, representatives of Great Britain, Canada, Australia, New Zealand and the Union of South Africa; the exiled governments of Belgium,

The League of Nations at its opening session in Geneva. ■ UN PHOTO/JULLIEN

Czechoslovakia, Greece, Luxembourg, the Netherlands, Norway, Poland and Yugoslavia; and General de Gaulle, leader of the Free French, met at the ancient St. James's Palace and signed a declaration, which states:

> "The only true basis of enduring peace is the willing cooperation of free peoples in a world in which, relieved of the menace of aggression, all may enjoy economic and social security; It is our intention to work together, and with other free peoples, both in war and peace, to this end."
>
> *Declaration of St. James's Palace*

The Atlantic Charter

Two months later, United States President Franklin D. Roosevelt and British Prime Minister Winston Churchill met somewhere at sea—the same sea on which the desperate Battle of the Atlantic was being fought—and on 14 August 1941, issued a joint declaration known in history as the Atlantic Charter.

In eight main points, the Atlantic Charter outlined a vision for a post-war settlement:

- No territorial gains were to be sought by the United States or the United Kingdom.
- Territorial adjustments must be in accord with the wishes of the peoples concerned.
- All peoples had a right to self-determination.
- Trade barriers were to be lowered.
- There was to be global economic cooperation and advancement of social welfare.
- Participants would work for a world free of want and fear.
- Participants would work for freedom of the seas.
- There was to be disarmament of aggressor nations and a post-war common disarmament.

DID YOU KNOW

Nobody ever signed the Atlantic Charter

No signed version of the Atlantic Charter ever existed. It took several drafts before the British War Cabinet and Washington telegraphed each other the final agreed-upon text.

At a press conference in December 1944, United States President Roosevelt admitted that "nobody signed the Atlantic Charter." In British Prime Minister Churchill's account of the Yalta Conference, he quotes Roosevelt as saying, of the unwritten British constitution, "it was like the Atlantic Charter—the document did not exist, yet all the world knew about it."

It should be noted that the document emphasized that both "victor [and] vanquished" would be given market access "on equal terms". This was a direct refusal to weaken the defeated nations' economies with punitive sanctions, like those that had been imposed on Germany after the First World War and that are believed to have been partially responsible for igniting the Second World War.

At the subsequent meeting of the Inter-Allied Council in St. James' Palace in London on 24 September 1941, the governments of Belgium, Czechoslovakia, Greece, Luxembourg, the Netherlands, Norway, Poland, the Soviet Union, Yugoslavia and representatives of General de Gaulle unanimously adopted adherence to the common principles of policy set forth in the Atlantic Charter.

Declaration by United Nations

On New Year's Day 1942, representatives of the United States, the United Kingdom, the Soviet Union and China signed a short document known as the Declaration by United Nations. The next day, representatives of 22 other nations added their signatures. This important document pledged the signatory governments to the maximum war effort and bound them against making a separate peace.

Three years later, when preparations were being made for the San Francisco Conference, only those States that had declared war on the Axis powers and subscribed to the Declaration by United Nations by March 1945 were invited to take part.

Signing of the Declaration by United Nations (1 January 1942). ■ UN PHOTO

Moscow and Tehran conferences

By 1943, the Allies were committed to creating a world in which people "in all lands may live out their lives in freedom from fear and want." But the basis for a world organization had yet to be defined. On 30 October 1943, Vyacheslav Molotov, Anthony Eden and Cordell Hull—foreign ministers of, respectively, the Soviet Union, the United Kingdom and the United States—together with Foo Ping Shen, the Chinese Ambassador to the Soviet Union, signed the Moscow Declaration, which "recognizes the necessity of establishing at the earliest practicable date a general international organization, based on the principle of the sovereign equality of all peace-loving States, and open to membership by all such States, large and small, for the maintenance of international peace and security."

In December 1943, the American, British and Soviet leaders, Roosevelt, Churchill and Stalin, met in Tehran, the capital of Iran, and declared that they had worked out concerted plans for final victory.

Dumbarton Oaks and Yalta

The principles of the world organization-to-be were thus laid down. The structure was discussed at a business-like conference at Dumbarton Oaks (Washington, D.C.) in the autumn of 1944 by representatives of China, the United Kingdom, the Soviet Union and the United States. On 7 October 1944, the four powers submitted a proposal for the framework of the world organization to all the United Nations governments and to the peoples of all countries for their study and discussion.

According to the Dumbarton Oaks proposals, four main bodies were to constitute the organization to be known as the United Nations:

- A General Assembly composed of all the members, with an Economic and Social Council working under its authority.
- A Security Council of 11 members, five permanent and six chosen from the remaining members by the General Assembly to hold office for two years.
- An International Court of Justice.
- A permanent Secretariat.

The essence of the plan was that the Security Council would be responsible for preventing future wars. The General Assembly would study, discuss and make recommendations in order to promote international cooperation and adjust situations likely to impair welfare. It would consider problems of cooperation in maintaining peace, security and disarmament. However, it would not make recommendations on any matter being considered by the Security Council.

Another important feature of the Dumbarton Oaks plan was that Member States were to place armed forces at the disposal of the Security Council in its task of preventing war and suppressing acts of aggression. The absence of

MORE INFO

We can build a better world

"The Charter of the United Nations which you have just signed is a solid structure upon which we can build a better world. History will honour you for it. Between the victory in Europe and the final victory, in this most destructive of all wars, you have won a victory against war itself. [...] With this Charter the world can begin to look forward to the time when all worthy human beings may be permitted to live decently as free people.

"If we fail to use it, we shall betray all those who have died so that we might meet here in freedom and safety to create it. If we seek to use it selfishly—for the advantage of any one nation or any small group of nations—we shall be equally guilty of that betrayal."

HARRY S. TRUMAN
President of the United States of America,
at the San Francisco Conference

such force, the organizers generally agreed, had been a fatal weakness in the League of Nations machinery for preserving peace.

The actual method of voting in the Security Council—an all-important question—was left open at Dumbarton Oaks for future discussion. It was taken up at Yalta (Crimea), where Churchill, Roosevelt and Stalin, together with their foreign ministers and chiefs of staff, again met in conference. On 11 February 1945, they announced that this question had been resolved and summoned the San Francisco Conference.

The San Francisco Conference: towards world peace

In the spring of 1945, delegates from 50 nations gathered in San Francisco. Together, they were representing over 80 per cent of the world's population and were determined to set up an organization that would preserve peace and help build a better world.

DID YOU KNOW

The term "United Nations" was first used by an American president

The name "United Nations" was suggested by United States President Franklin D. Roosevelt.

It was first officially used in 1942, when representatives of 26 countries signed the Declaration by United Nations.

As a tribute to President Roosevelt, who died a few weeks before the signing of the Charter, all those present at the San Francisco Conference agreed to adopt the name "United Nations".

The main objective of the San Francisco Conference was to produce a document acceptable to all countries that would guide the work of the new organization.

The Charter, the guiding principles of the United Nations, was signed on 26 June 1945, by the representatives of these 50 countries.

Poland was not represented at the Conference, because at that time, the country did not yet have a new government in place. However, Poland signed the Charter by 15 October 1945 and is therefore considered one of the original Members of the United Nations.

The 51 original Members States were (in alphabetical order, using the names of the countries as they were known in October 1945):

1. Argentina	18. El Salvador	36. Panama
2. Australia	19. Ethiopia	37. Paraguay
3. Belgium	20. France	38. Peru
4. Bolivia	21. Greece	39. Philippine Republic
5. Brazil	22. Guatemala	40. Poland
6. Byelorussian Soviet Socialist Republic	23. Haiti	41. Saudi Arabia
7. Canada	24. Honduras	42. Syria
8. Chile	25. India	43. Turkey
9. China	26. Iran	44. Ukrainian Soviet Socialist Republic
10. Colombia	27. Iraq	45. Union of South Africa
11. Costa Rica	28. Lebanon	46. Union of Soviet Socialist Republics (USSR)
12. Cuba	29. Liberia	47. United Kingdom (UK)
13. Czechoslovakia	30. Luxembourg	48. United States of America (USA)
14. Denmark	31. Mexico	49. Uruguay
15. Dominican Republic	32. Netherlands	50. Venezuela
16. Ecuador	33. New Zealand	51. Yugoslavia
17. Egypt	34. Nicaragua	
	35. Norway	

After the represented countries, including the five permanent members of the Security Council (China, France, USA, UK and USSR), signed the Charter of the United Nations and officially recognized it, the United Nations came into being on 24 October 1945.

WHAT IS THE UNITED NATIONS?

The United Nations is a unique organization composed of independent countries that have come together to work for world peace and social progress. The Organization formally came into existence with just 51 countries. By 2017, the membership of the United Nations had grown to 193 countries.

Since its inception, no country has ever been expelled from the United Nations. Indonesia temporarily quit the Organization in 1965 over a dispute with neighbouring Malaysia but returned the following year.

A forum for countries, not a world government

Governments represent countries and peoples. The United Nations represents neither a particular government nor any one nation. It represents all its Members and does only what the Member States decide that it should do.

Guiding principles of the United Nations

The Charter of the United Nations is the founding document guiding all of its undertakings. It is a set of guidelines that explains the rights and duties of each Member State and what needs to be done to achieve the goals they have set for themselves. When a nation becomes a Member of the United Nations, it accepts the aims and rules of the Charter.

FOCUS ON

The road to the United Nations

28 June 1919	Creation of the League of Nations
3 September 1939	Poland invaded: Britain and France declare war on German Reich
7 December 1941	Attack on Pearl Harbour: the United States of America joins the Allies
12 June 1941	Declaration of St. James's Palace
14 August 1941	Adoption of the Atlantic Charter
1-2 January 1942	Declaration by United Nations
October-December 1943	Moscow and Tehran Conferences
Summer/autumn 1944	Dumbarton Oaks proposals
11 February 1945	Yalta Conference
8 May 1945	Allied victory in Europe proclaimed
26 June 1945	Adoption of the Charter of the United Nations at San Francisco Conference
24 October 1945	Creation of the United Nations
10 January 1946	First session of the United Nations General Assembly in London with representatives of 51 nations

The United Nations flag. ■ UN PHOTO/JOHN ISAAC

Emblem

The original emblem was designed for the San Francisco Conference. After slight modifications, it was approved on 7 December 1946, as the emblem of the United Nations.

The design is a map of the world surrounded by a wreath consisting of crossed olive branches. The world map is centred on the North Pole and extends to 60 degrees south latitude: this projection allows for all countries to be displayed with none at the centre, representing the equality of all nations. The olive branches symbolize peace.

The original colours were gold on a field of smoke-blue with all water areas in white.

Flag

The official flag of the United Nations was adopted on 20 October 1947. It consists of the official emblem of the United Nations in white on a blue background. The emblem is one half the height of the flag and entirely centred.

DID YOU KNOW

The United Nations has four main purposes

- ▪ To keep peace throughout the world.
- ▪ To develop friendly relations among nations.
- ▪ To improve the lives of poor people, to eradicate hunger, disease and illiteracy and to encourage respect for each other's rights and freedoms.
- ▪ To be a centre for helping nations achieve these goals.

STRUCTURE OF THE ORGANIZATION

The work of the United Nations is carried out almost all over the world by six principal organs:

- General Assembly
- Security Council
- Economic and Social Council
- Trusteeship Council
- International Court of Justice
- Secretariat

All these organs are based at United Nations Headquarters in New York, except for the International Court of Justice, which is located at The Hague, Netherlands.

There are 15 specialized agencies that coordinate their work with the United Nations. In addition, there are 24 United Nations programmes, funds, institutes and other bodies with responsibilities in specific fields. All in all, the United Nations family of organizations focuses on areas as diverse as health, food and agriculture, telecommunications, tourism, labour, postal services, the environment, civil aviation, children, atomic energy, cultural preservation, science, refugees, intellectual property, gender equality, drugs, crime and terrorism, human settlements, maritime transport and weather. All these various bodies work together with the United Nations Secretariat and compose the United Nations System.

UNITED NATIONS HEADQUARTERS

The United Nations Headquarters in New York is an international zone. This means that the land on which the United Nations sits does not belong to just the United States, the host country, but to all the Members. The United Nations has its own flag and its own security officers who guard the area. It also has its own post office and issues its own stamps. United Nations stamps can be used only from United Nations Headquarters or from United Nations offices at Geneva and Vienna. The compound has its own bookshop, which specializes in UN affairs and related topics.

MEMBERSHIP AND BUDGET

The United Nations has three distinct budget lines:

- The regular budget, for core functions at Headquarters in New York, major regional offices at Geneva, Nairobi and Vienna, and a range of field offices in different continents.

The United Nations Headquarters in New York today. ■ UN PHOTO

- The peacekeeping budget, to cover the cost of peacekeeping operations, often in war-torn zones, around the world.

- The budget for the International Criminal Tribunal for Rwanda, situated in Arusha, Tanzania, and the International Criminal Tribunal for the Former Yugoslavia, situated in The Hague, Netherlands.

An iconic building

At its first meeting in London in 1946, the United Nations General Assembly decided to locate the United Nations Headquarters in the United States. Philadelphia, Boston, Chicago, San Francisco, etc. were all considered to host the United Nations Headquarters. What eventually persuaded the General Assembly to settle on the present site was a last-minute gift of $8.5 million from John D. Rockefeller, Jr. Later, New York City offered additional property as a gift.

In the mid-1940s, the site chosen for the United Nations Headquarters was a rather derelict zone of slaughterhouses, a railroad garage and other commercial buildings.

On 24 October 1949, United Nations Secretary-General Trygve Lie laid the cornerstone of the 39-storey building. On 21 August 1950, the Secretariat's staff began moving into their new offices. The United Nations Headquarters buildings in New York were designed by an international team of 11 architects, including Oscar Niemeyer (Brazil) and Le Corbusier (Switzerland/France).

Payment to the United Nations for all types of budgets is compulsory. Members pay according to an agreed-upon scale of assessment. This scale, reviewed every three years, is based on a country's ability to pay, national income and population.

The specialized organizations that form part of the United Nations System have budgets separate from the four United Nations budgets described above. The bulk of their resources emanate from voluntary contributions by governments, individuals and institutions.

Largest contributors to the 2017 United Nations regular budget

MEMBER STATES	CONTRIBUTIONS (United States Dollars)	CONTRIBUTIONS (Percentage of the budget)
United States of America	610 836 578	22.0%
Japan	268 768 094	9.7%
China	219 928 933	7.9%
Germany	177 392 495	6.4%
France	134 911 588	4.9%
United Kingdom of Great Britain and Northern Ireland	123 916 530	4.5%
Brazil	106 146 738	3.8%
Italy	104 064 341	3.7%
Russian Federation	85 739 243	3.1%
Canada	81 102 438	2.9%
Spain	67 830 626	2.4%
Australia	64 887 504	2.3%
Republic of Korea	56 613 445	2.0%
Netherlands	41 148 173	1.5%
Mexico	39 843 204	1.4%

Source: www.un.org/en/ga/search/view_doc.asp?symbol=ST/ADM/SER.B/955

Top 10 financial providers to United Nations peacekeeping operations in 2017

1. United States of America	28.5%
2. China	10.3%
3. Japan	9.7%
4. Germany	6.4%
5. France	6.3%
6. United Kingdom of Great Britain and Northern Ireland	5.8%
7. Russian Federation	4.0%
8. Italy	3.8%
9. Canada	2.9%
10. Spain	2.4%
Other Member States	20.1%

Source: www.un.org/en/ga/search/view_doc.asp?symbol=A/70/331/Add.1

Good value for money

The regular budget for the United Nations is approved by the General Assembly for a two-year period. The budget approved for 2016-2017 is $5.4 billion, which pays for United Nations activities, staff and basic infrastructure.

For peacekeeping, the budget for the year from 1 July 2016 to 30 June 2017 was $7.87 billion. In comparison, every year, the world spends nearly $2 trillion on military expenditures. Peace is far cheaper than war and a good value for money.

Funding the United Nations (2017)

Most of the work of the United Nations is funded by contributions from all Member States. Additional funds come from commercial activities (guided tours, the sale of publications, databases, apps, etc.) or from a public or private entity that donates money to a trust fund managed by the United Nations for the purpose of a special project or programme.

Becoming a Member State of the United Nations

Membership, in accordance with the Charter of the United Nations, "is open to all peace-loving States that accept the obligations contained in the United Nations Charter and, in the judgment of the Organization, are able to carry out these obligations". States are admitted by decision of the General Assembly upon the recommendation of the Security Council.

In brief, the procedure is as follows:

- The requesting country or entity submits an application to the Secretary-General and a letter formally stating that it accepts the obligations under the Charter.

- The Security Council considers the application. Any recommendation for admission must receive affirmative votes from 9 of the 15 members of the Council, provided that none of its five permanent members—China, France, the Russian Federation, the United Kingdom and the United States of America—has voted against the application.

- If the Council recommends admission, the recommendation is presented to the General Assembly for consideration. A two-thirds majority vote is necessary in the Assembly for admission of a new State.

- Membership becomes effective on the day the resolution for admission is adopted.

Permanent Observer States

Non-Member States of the United Nations, which are members of one or more specialized agencies, can apply for the status of Permanent Observer. The status of a Permanent Observer is based purely on practice; there are no provisions for it in the United Nations Charter. The practice dates from 1946, when the Secretary-General accepted the designation of neutral Switzerland as a Permanent Observer to the United Nations. Switzerland became a Member State in 2002. By 2017, the Holy See (Vatican City) was the sole sovereign State with Permanent Observer status, and Palestine was the sole entity with such status.

Many regional and international organizations are also observers of the work and annual sessions of the General Assembly.

OFFICIAL LANGUAGES

The official languages used at the United Nations are Arabic, Chinese, English, French, Russian and Spanish. The working languages are English and French.

During meetings, delegates may speak in any of the official languages, and the speech is interpreted simultaneously in the other official languages. Most United Nations documents are also issued in all six official languages.

At times, a delegate may choose to make a statement using a non-official language. In such cases, the delegation must provide either an interpretation or a written text of the statement in one of the official languages.

DID YOU KNOW

Membership grew from 51 States in 1945 to 193 today

South Sudan officially broke away from Sudan on 9 July 2011.

On 17 July 2011, the General Assembly admitted the Republic of South Sudan as the 193rd member of the United Nations, welcoming the newly independent country to the world community.

South Sudan's national flag (fourth from left) flies at UN Headquarters following the admission of the country as the 193rd Member State. ■ UN PHOTO/J.C. MCILWAINE

Chapter 2

THE UNITED NATIONS FAMILY

QUICK FACTS ABOUT THE UNITED NATIONS FAMILY

■ The United Nations was initially conceived as a wartime alliance on 1 January 1942, and established as an international organization on 24 October 1945. To commemorate the creation of the United Nations, the world celebrates **United Nations Day** each year on 24 October.

■ The United Nations has **four purposes**: (1) to maintain international peace and security; (2) to develop friendly relations among nations; (3) to cooperate in solving international problems and promoting respect for human rights; and (4) to be a centre for harmonizing the actions of nations. More than 30 affiliated organizations cooperate in this effort. They are known together as the **United Nations System**, and all have their own specific areas of work.

■ The United Nations is **not a world government**. However, it does provide the means to help resolve international conflicts and formulate policies on matters affecting all of us. The United Nations is a forum where all countries meet to discuss, elaborate and extend international law in areas such as human rights, international trade, the sea, and the fight against terrorism.

■ At the United Nations, all the Member States—large and small, rich and poor, with differing political views and social systems— have a voice and a vote in making decisions in the **General Assembly**.

■ The United Nations System works to promote respect for human rights, reduce poverty, fight disease and protect the environment. The United Nations leads **international campaigns** against drug trafficking and terrorism, as well as to eliminate violence against women and to protect natural ecosystems.

■ The United Nations and its agencies undertake a myriad of **projects throughout the world**, including assisting refugees; fighting AIDS and malaria; expanding food production; protecting labour; supporting education for all, and providing help in the wake of natural disasters and armed conflicts.

PRINCIPAL ORGANS OF THE UNITED NATIONS

The Charter establishes six principal organs of the United Nations. This is a summary of their composition and functions.

General Assembly

All members of the United Nations (currently 193 States) are represented in the General Assembly. Each nation, rich or poor, large or small, has one vote:

- China, which has 1,379 billion inhabitants, gets one vote; so does Tuvalu, with its 11,097 inhabitants (2016).
- The largest country in the world, the Russian Federation, has one vote, just like the Principality of Monaco, which is roughly the size of New York City's Central Park.

A Member State can lose its vote if it fails to pay its dues and owes the Organization an amount equal to or exceeding the contributions due for two preceding years. An exception is allowed if the Member State can show that conditions beyond its control contributed to this inability to pay.

In the General Assembly, decisions on such issues as international peace and security, admission of new Member States and the United Nations budget are decided by a two-thirds majority. Other matters require only a simple majority. In recent years, a special effort has been made to reach decisions through consensus, rather than by taking a formal vote.

The General Assembly Hall accommodates all delegations. Each delegation has six seats, and there is a gallery for the media and the public, making a total of 1,898 seats. ■ UN PHOTO/MARCO CASTRO

The General Assembly's regular session begins on Tuesday in the third week of September and continues throughout the year. At the beginning of each regular session, the Assembly holds a general debate at which Heads of State or Government and others present views on a wide-ranging agenda of issues of concern to the international community, from war and terrorism to disease and poverty.

Each year, the General Assembly elects a President who presides over the meetings. To ensure equitable geographical representation, the presidency rotates among five groups of countries:

- African States
- Asian States
- Eastern European States
- Latin American and Caribbean States
- Western European and other States

Functions

The General Assembly is the principal organ that:

- Discusses and makes recommendations on any subject, except those being considered at the same time by the Security Council.
- Discusses questions related to military conflicts and the arms race.
- Discusses ways and means to improve the status of children, refugees, women and many others.
- Discusses issues related to sustainable development and human rights.
- Decides how much each Member State should pay to the United Nations and how this money is spent.

Main Committees

Because of the overwhelming number of questions it is called upon to consider, the General Assembly allocates items among its six Main Committees and other subsidiary organs. The Committees and organs discuss the issues, seeking as much as possible to harmonize the various positions different countries may have, and then present to a plenary (full) meeting of the Assembly draft resolutions and decisions for consideration.

The six Main Committees are:

- The First Committee, which deals with issues of disarmament and international security.
- The Second Committee, which specializes in economic and financial questions.

- The Third Committee, which focuses on social, humanitarian and cultural topics.
- The Fourth Committee, which addresses special political issues and questions relating to decolonization.
- The Fifth Committee, which works on administrative and budgetary questions.
- The Sixth Committee, which reviews legal issues.

Examples of recent action by the General Assembly

- In September 2015, the 193 Member States of the United Nations adopted the historic 2030 Sustainable Development Agenda, which outlines 17 Sustainable Development Goals (SDGs) and the associated 169 targets to be met globally by 2030. The SDGs build upon the Millennium Development Goals (MDGs) that were adopted by the General Assembly in 2000.
- In December 2010, the General Assembly declared 2011-2020 the United Nations Decade on Biodiversity. Protecting biodiversity is in our self-interest. Biological resources are the pillars upon which we build civilizations. The loss of biodiversity threatens our food supplies, our opportunities for recreation and tourism and our sources of wood, medicines and energy. It also interferes with essential ecological functions.
- In July 2010, the General Assembly created UN-Women, a historic step towards the realization of the Organization's goals on gender equality and the empowerment of women. UN-Women brings together the resources and mandates of four previously distinct UN entities for greater impact. Empowering women sparks progress in education, health, productivity and the economy, and therefore boosts a country's level of development.

Security Council

While the General Assembly can discuss any world concern, the Security Council is primarily responsible for questions of peace and security.

Functions

The Security Council is the principal organ that:

- Investigates any dispute or situation that might lead to international conflict.
- Recommends methods and terms of settlement.
- Recommends actions against any threat or act of aggression.
- Recommends to the General Assembly who should be appointed as Secretary- General of the United Nations.

The Security Council chamber, a gift from Norway, was designed by Norwegian artist Arnstein Arneberg. A large mural by Per Krohg (Norway), symbolizing the promise of future peace and individual freedom, covers most of the east wall. ■ UN PHOTO/RIAK BAJORNAS

Membership

The Security Council has 15 members. Five are permanent members: China, France, the Russian Federation, the United Kingdom and the United States. The other 10 non- permanent members are elected by the General Assembly for two-year terms and are chosen on the basis of geographical representation.

Some Member States have been advocating for changes in the membership of the Security Council. They want to increase the number of permanent members to include more of the world's largest countries, and they argue that African issues represent 70 per cent of the Security Council's work, yet the continent still lacks permanent representation.

Meetings

The Security Council, unlike the General Assembly, does not hold regular meetings. Instead, it can be called to meet at any given time and on very short

DID YOU KNOW

Five countries have the right to veto

At the end of the Second World War, China, France, the Soviet Union (which was succeeded in 1990 by the Russian Federation), the United Kingdom and the United States played key roles in the establishment of the United Nations. The creators of the United Nations Charter thought that these five countries would continue to play important roles in the maintenance of international peace and security. So the "big five" were given a special voting power unofficially known as the "right to veto." The drafters agreed that if any one of the "big five" cast a negative vote in the 15-member Security Council, the resolution or decision would not be approved.

notice. Members take turns being President of the Security Council for a month at a time. They serve in the English-language alphabetical order of the names of the Member States they represent.

To pass a resolution in the Security Council, 9 out of the 15 members must vote "yes"; however, if any of the five permanent members votes "no"—such a vote is often referred to as a veto—the resolution does not pass.

Examples of action taken by the Security Council

In March 2016, the Security Council unanimously adopted new sanctions in response to North Korea's nuclear tests and its launch of long-range missiles. In March 2017, the Council extended the monitoring of the sanctions regime.

In July 2011, following the declaration of independence of South Sudan, the Council established the United Nations Mission in the Republic of South Sudan (UNMISS), in an attempt to foster peace and security and to create favourable conditions for development in the new country.

The Council established two international criminal tribunals to prosecute those responsible for war crimes and crimes against humanity in the former Yugoslavia and in Rwanda during the 1990s.

Following the terrorist attacks on the United States on 11 September 2001, the Council established its Counter-Terrorism Committee to help States increase their capability to combat terrorism.

Economic and Social Council (ECOSOC)

The Economic and Social Council (ECOSOC) is the forum for discussion of economic questions, such as trade, transport and economic development, and social issues, such as poverty and better livelihoods. It also helps countries reach agreements on how to improve education and health conditions and how to promote respect for, and observance of, universal human rights and freedoms of people everywhere.

Functions

The ECOSOC is the principal organ that:

- Promotes higher standards of living, full employment, and economic and social progress.

- Identifies solutions to international economic, social and health problems.

- Facilitates international cultural and educational cooperation.

- Encourages universal respect for human rights and fundamental freedoms.

The ECOSOC has the power to make or initiate studies and reports on these issues. It is also involved in the preparation and organization of major international conferences in the economic, social and related fields and is involved in the practical follow-ups to these conferences.

Membership

The ECOSOC has 54 members that serve for three-year terms. Voting in the Council is by simple majority; each member has one vote.

Each year, the ECOSOC holds several short sessions focused on the planning of its own work, often including representatives of civil society. The Council also holds an annual four-week "substantive" session in July to discuss matters of major or practical importance to all concerned countries, alternating the venue between Geneva and New York.

Subsidiary Bodies

The ECOSOC has a variety of thematic commissions to administer the wide range of issues that fall within its purview, including:

- The Commission on Narcotic Drugs.
- The Commission for Social Development.
- The Commission on Population and Development.
- The Statistical Commission.
- The Commission on Crime Prevention and Criminal Justice.
- The Commission on the Status of Women.
- The Commission on Science and Technology for Development.
- The United Nations Forum on Forests.

The Council also directs five regional commissions:

- The Economic Commission for Africa (ECA).
- The Economic Commission for Europe (ECE), which also covers the countries of North America and the former USSR.
- The Economic Commission for Latin America and the Caribbean (ECLAC).
- The Economic and Social Commission for Asia and the Pacific (ESCAP).
- The Economic and Social Commission for Western Asia (ESCWA), which covers the Arab countries located in Asia and north Africa.

Trusteeship Council

In 1945, when the United Nations was established, 11 non-self-governing territories (mostly in Africa and the Pacific Ocean) were placed under international supervision. The major goals of the trusteeship system were to promote the

FOCUS ON

Decolonization

In 1945, half of the world's people lived in countries that were governed from outside. These countries, known as colonies, were controlled by a handful of major, mostly—but not only—European powers. Through the process known as decolonization, the United Nations has helped the colonies gain independence. The General Assembly, in 1960, adopted a declaration to urge the speedy independence of all colonies and peoples. The following year, it set up a Special Committee on Decolonization. As a result of the United Nations' efforts, more than 80 former colonies are now themselves members of the Organization.

Today, about one million people live in dependent territories. Many of the territories—for the most part small or isolated islands—wish to remain associated with their outside administering powers and have established autonomous local institutions to manage their own affairs. However, after the withdrawal of Spain as administering power in 1976, the question of the status of Western Sahara has yet to be resolved. This remains a focus of United Nations attention, with the United Nations Mission for the Referendum in Western Sahara (MINURSO) established in 1991. A referendum under discussion would invite the territory's inhabitants to decide if they desire full independence as a sovereign State or integration with Morocco.

advancement of the inhabitants of such Trust Territories and their progression towards self-government or independence.

Membership

The Trusteeship Council is composed of the permanent members of the Security Council (China, France, the Russian Federation, the United Kingdom and the United States). Each member has one vote, and decisions are made by a simple majority.

Meetings

Since the last Trust Territory—Palau, formerly administered by the United States—achieved self-government in 1994 and became a Member State of the United Nations, the Council formally suspended operations after nearly half a century. It may meet again if the need arises.

International Court of Justice

The International Court of Justice, also known as the World Court, was established by the Charter of the United Nations in 1945 and began its work in April 1946. The seat of the Court is at the Peace Palace in The Hague

(Netherlands). Of the six principal organs of the United Nations, it is the only one not located in New York.

Functions

The Court is the principal organ that:

- Settles legal disputes submitted by States in accordance with international law.
- Gives advisory opinions on legal questions referred by authorized United Nations organs and specialized agencies.

States bring disputes before the Court in search of impartial solutions to their differences with other countries. By achieving peaceful settlement on such questions as land frontiers, maritime boundaries and territorial sovereignty, the Court has often helped prevent the escalation of disputes into larger conflicts that could lead to loss of life.

All judgments passed by the Court are final and cannot be appealed.

Membership

The Court is composed of 15 judges elected by the General Assembly and the Security Council. No two judges can be from the same country, and it takes a majority of nine judges to make a decision. The Court is assisted by a Registry, its administrative organ.

After an international competition, French architect Louis Cordonnier won the design of the Peace Palace in The Hague, Netherlands. It has housed the International Court of Justice and its predecessors since 1913. ■ UN PHOTO

Cases and Advisory Opinions

In its judgments, the Court has addressed international disputes involving economic rights, environmental protection, rights of passage, the use of force, interference in the internal affairs of States, diplomatic relations, hostage-taking, the right of asylum and nationality.

From 1946 to 2017, the International Court of Justice had considered some 165 cases, issued numerous judgments on disputes brought to it by States and issued advisory opinions in response to requests by a range of United Nations organizations. The number of cases submitted to the Court has increased significantly since the 1970s, when it decided only one or two cases at any given time. In 2017, there were 15 cases pending in the Court, including one (*Ukraine v. Russian Federation*) under active consideration.

The Court's advisory opinions have dealt with, among other things, membership admission to the United Nations, reparation for injuries suffered in the service of the United Nations, the territorial status of Western Sahara and the legality of the threat or use of nuclear weapons.

Secretariat

The Secretariat, headed by the Secretary-General, consists of staff representing nationalities from all over the world. They carry out the day-to-day work of the United Nations; their duties are as varied as the problems dealt with by the Organization. These range from administering peacekeeping operations to mediating international disputes to surveying social and economic trends. The Secretariat serves the other organs of the United Nations and is responsible for administering the programmes and policies laid down by them.

Functions

The Secretariat is the principal organ that:

- Administers peacekeeping operations, mediates international disputes and organizes humanitarian relief programmes.
- Surveys economic and social trends, prepares studies on human rights, sustainable development and other areas of concern, and produces a variety of publications.
- Lays the groundwork for international agreements.
- Informs the world—the media, governments, non-governmental organizations, research and academic networks, schools and colleges and the general public—about the work of the United Nations.
- Assists in carrying out the decisions of the United Nations.
- Organizes international conferences on subjects of vital concern for humankind.
- Interprets speeches and translates documents into the six official languages of the United Nations.

The Office of the High Commissioner for Human Rights

The Office of the United Nations High Commissioner for Human Rights (OHCHR) is not a United Nations agency but an integral part of the United Nations Secretariat. Headquartered in Geneva, it represents the world's commitment to universal ideals of human dignity. OHCHR works with all governments to help promote and implement human rights worldwide.

OHCHR provides expertise and technical training in the administration of justice, legislative reform and electoral process, to help implement international human rights standards around the world.

OHCHR also assists other entities with the protection of human rights; helps all women, children and men realize their rights and legitimate aspirations; and speaks out in the face of human rights violations committed by State and non-State actors. There are still many human rights violations taking place today, which necessitate the independent and objective scrutiny of the United Nations.

Secretary-General

The Charter of the United Nations describes the Secretary-General as the chief administrative officer of the Organization, who shall act in this capacity and perform "functions as are entrusted" to him or her by the General Assembly, Security Council, Economic and Social Council and other United Nations organs.

The Secretary-General is assisted by staff from all countries—people referred to as "international civil servants." Unlike traditional diplomats, who represent a particular country and its interests, international civil servants work for all 193 Member States and take their orders not from governments but from the Secretary-General. They are independent from political and other forms of interference and place the interests of the Organization above their own.

The Secretary-General does not act alone

The Secretary-General does not act without the support and approval of the United Nations Member States.

Any course of action, whether it concerns sending peacekeeping troops to war-torn areas or helping a country rebuild after a war or a natural disaster, must be set by the Member States.

ROLE OF THE SECRETARY-GENERAL

The Secretary-General:

- Proposes issues to be discussed by the General Assembly or any other organ of the United Nations.
- Brings to the attention of the Security Council any problem that he or she feels may threaten world peace.
- Acts as a "referee" in disputes between Member States.

FOCUS ON

António Guterres, Secretary-General

António Guterres, the ninth Secretary-General of the United Nations, took office on 1 January 2017.

Having witnessed the suffering of the most vulnerable people on earth in refugee camps and in war zones, Mr. Guterres resolved to make human dignity the core of his work and to serve as a peace broker, a bridge-builder and a promoter of reform and innovation.

Mr. Guterres served as **United Nations High Commissioner for Refugees (UNHCR)** from June 2005 to December 2015, heading one of the world's foremost humanitarian organizations during some of the most serious displacement crises in decades. Today's conflicts have led to a huge rise in UNHCR's activities, as the number of people displaced rose from 38 million in 2005 to over 65 million in 2017.

Before joining UNHCR, Mr. Guterres spent more than 20 years in government and public service. He served as prime minister of Portugal from 1995 to 2002, during which time he was heavily involved in the international effort to resolve the crisis in East Timor.

As president of the European Council in early 2000, he led the adoption of the Lisbon Agenda for growth and jobs, and co-chaired the first European Union-Africa summit. He was a member of the Portuguese Council of State from 1991 to 2002.

Mr. Guterres was elected to the Portuguese Parliament in 1976, where he served as a member for 17 years. During that time, he chaired the Parliamentary Committee for Economy, Finance and Planning, and later the Parliamentary Committee for Territorial Administration, Municipalities and Environment. He was also leader of his party's parliamentary group.

From 1981 to 1983, Mr. Guterres was a member of the Parliamentary Assembly of the Council of Europe, where he chaired the Committee on Demography, Migration and Refugees.

■ Offers his or her "good offices"—steps taken publicly and in private, drawing upon the Secretary-General's independence, impartiality and integrity, as well as his or her prestige and the weight of the international community, to prevent international disputes from arising, escalating or spreading.

APPOINTMENT OF THE SECRETARY-GENERAL

The Secretary-General is appointed for a period of five years by the General Assembly on the recommendation of the Security Council. There have been nine Secretaries-General since the United Nations was created. The appointment of the Secretary-General follows a regional rotation.

UNITED NATIONS SECRETARIES-GENERAL

Those who have served as Secretary-General since the creation of the United Nations are:

Trygve Lie (Norway)
1946-1952

Dag Hammarskjöld (Sweden)
1953-1961

U Thant (Burma)
1961-1971

Kurt Waldheim (Austria)
1972-1981

Javier Pérez de Cuéllar (Peru)
1982-1991

Boutros Boutros-Ghali (Egypt)
1992-1996

Kofi Annan (Ghana)
1997-2006

Ban Ki-moon (South Korea)
2007-2016

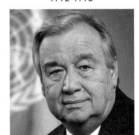

António Guterres (Portugal)
2017-present

Four main offices

UNITED NATIONS HEADQUARTERS IN NEW YORK (UNHQ)

The United Nations Headquarters in New York (United States of America) by the numbers:

- 193 diplomatic delegations representing Member States, who send more than 5,000 people to New York each year for the annual sessions of the General Assembly.
- About 5,500 international staff members.
- One million visitors touring the Headquarters every year.
- 2,000 journalists permanently accredited and nearly 3,500 present during major events and meetings.
- More than 5,000 non-governmental organizations accredited to the United Nations.

*United Nations Headquarters
in New York* ■ UN PHOTO

*United Nations Office
at Geneva* ■ UN PHOTO/FERRÉ

*United Nations Office
at Nairobi* ■ UN PHOTO

*United Nations Office
at Vienna* ■ UN PHOTO/GARTEN

United Nations Office at Geneva (UNOG)

The United Nations Office at Geneva (Switzerland), the European regional headquarters, serves as the base for the United Nations Conference on Trade and Development (UNCTAD), the Office of the High-Commissioner for Human Rights (OHCHR) and the Economic Commission for Europe (UNECE) among others.

The United Nations office at Geneva by the numbers:

- 184 diplomatic delegations representing Member States.
- Around 8,500 staff members working for the United Nations and its specialized agencies, funds and programmes.
- About 100,000 visitors touring the Palais des Nations every year.
- 230 journalists permanently accredited.
- Hundreds of non-governmental organizations accredited to the United Nations.
- Approximately 9,960 meetings organized every year.

United Nations Office at Nairobi (UNON)

The United Nations Office at Nairobi (Kenya) serves as the global headquarters of the United Nations Environment (UNEP) and the United Nations Programme for Human Settlements (UN-Habitat).

The United Nations Office at Nairobi by the numbers:

- 146 diplomatic delegations representing Member States.
- 2,800 staff working at UNEP and UN-Habitat.
- An array of diplomatic gatherings and peacebuilding initiatives.
- Hundreds of people working for non-governmental organizations accredited to the United Nations.

United Nations Office at Vienna (UNOV)

The United Nations Office at Vienna (Austria) serves as headquarters for the International Atomic Energy Agency (IAEA), the United Nations Industrial Development Organization (UNIDO), the United Nations Office for Outer Space Affairs (UNOOSA) and the United Nations Office on Drugs and Crime (UNODC).

The United Nations Office at Vienna by the numbers:

- Dozens of diplomatic delegations representing Member States.
- 4,000 employees working for the Vienna-based United Nations organizations.
- Approximately 2,000 international conferences and meetings held annually.

FOCUS ON

About the Regional Offices

THE PALAIS DES NATIONS

The United Nations Office at Geneva building previously hosted the headquarters of the League of Nations, the precursor to the United Nations. At the end of the Second World War, the League gave way to the United Nations, which inherited its physical assets, including an imposing architectural edifice referred to as the Palais des Nations (Palace of Nations).

THE UNITED NATIONS AND KENYA

The United Nations has heavily invested in wildlife conservation, forest restoration and ecotourism, all of which provide unquantifiable economic benefits for local residents. It has supported thousands of community-based projects, touching hundreds of thousands of lives in Kenya.

"UNITED NATIONS CITY" IN VIENNA

The United Nations Office at Vienna, also known as the Vienna International Centre (VIC), opened in August 1979. The six Y-shaped office towers were designed to let staff work in natural sunlight rather than artificial light in almost every office. Locally, the Vienna International Centre, which is situated on the outskirts of the Austrian capital, is often referred to as "United Nations City."

THE UNITED NATIONS: A FAMILY OF SPECIALIZED ENTITIES

There are 15 specialized agencies and 24 programmes, funds and other bodies with specific responsibilities all related to the United Nations. These programmes and bodies, together with the United Nations itself, compose the United Nations System.

The various entities belonging to the United Nations system are listed below by type of organization, and in alphabetical order within each type.

Agencies

FOOD AND AGRICULTURE ORGANIZATION (FAO)

The Food and Agriculture Organization works to eradicate hunger and malnutrition and to raise levels of nutrition. It also assists Member States in the sustainable development of agriculture, forestry and fisheries, helping them move towards achieving food security. Combating hunger and malnutrition has important indirect effects on children, such as reducing child labour, allowing to attend school and improving their health.

International Civil Aviation Organization (ICAO)

The International Civil Aviation Organization assures the safe, secure, orderly and sustainable development of international air transport while minimizing the adverse effect of global civil aviation on the environment. In an effort to combat child trafficking, it recommends that all countries require a separate passport for each child.

International Fund for Agricultural Development (IFAD)

The International Fund for Agricultural Development is dedicated to eradicating rural poverty in developing countries. About 75 per cent of the world's poorest people—that is, about one billion women, children and men—live in rural areas and depend on agriculture and related activities for their livelihoods. IFAD invests in agriculture and rural development projects that reach poor, marginalized and vulnerable people in rural areas and helps create the conditions they need to improve their lives.

International Labour Organization (ILO)

The International Labour Organization formulates policies and programmes to promote the basic human rights of workers, improve working and living conditions and enhance employment opportunities. It also leads efforts to eradicate child labour worldwide.

International Maritime Organization (IMO)

The International Maritime Organization is responsible for improving the safety and security of international shipping and for preventing marine pollution from ships. It is also involved in legal matters such as liability and compensation issues and the facilitation of international maritime traffic.

International Monetary Fund (IMF)

The International Monetary Fund promotes the stability of the global monetary and financial system. It advises on key economic policies, provides temporary financial assistance and training, promotes growth and strives to alleviate poverty.

International Telecommunications Union (ITU)

The International Telecommunications Union is committed to connecting the world. The global international telecommunications network is one of the largest and most sophisticated engineering feats ever accomplished, and ITU is at its very heart. ITU negotiates agreements on technologies, services and allocation of global resources like radio-frequency spectrum and satellite orbital positions, creating a seamless global communications system that is robust, reliable and constantly evolving.

United Nations Educational, Scientific and Cultural Organization (UNESCO)

The United Nations Educational, Scientific and Cultural Organization promotes international cooperation and facilitates the exchange of information in the fields of education, science, culture and communications. It works to safeguard the world's cultural heritage. It aims to empower, educate and inspire young people, and seeks to preserve the cultural and natural heritage of humanity.

United Nations Industrial Development Organization (UNIDO)

The United Nations Industrial Development Organization promotes and accelerates sustainable industrial growth in developing countries and economies in transition. It aims to give each country an opportunity to create a flourishing productive sector, increase its participation in international trade and safeguard its environment.

UNIVERSAL POSTAL UNION (UPU)

The Universal Postal Union sets the rules for international mail exchanges. It makes recommendations to stimulate growth in mail, parcel and financial services and to improve the quality of service for customers. It also provides technical assistance where needed.

WORLD BANK

The World Bank aims to overcome poverty, enhance economic growth while caring for the environment and create individual opportunities and hope. To this end, it provides low-interest loans, interest-free credits and grants to developing countries to be invested in education, health, public administration, infrastructure, financial and private-sector development, agriculture and environmental and natural resource management.

WORLD HEALTH ORGANIZATION (WHO)

The World Health Organization is responsible for providing leadership on global health matters, shaping the health research agenda and setting norms and standards. Today, health is a shared responsibility, involving equitable access to essential care and collective protection against transboundary epidemic threats. Special emphasis is given to children's health, since they are more vulnerable to malnutrition and infectious diseases, many of which are preventable and treatable.

WORLD INTELLECTUAL PROPERTY ORGANIZATION (WIPO)

The World Intellectual Property Organization ensures that the rights of creators and owners of intellectual property—people such as musicians, writers, scientists and inventors—are protected worldwide and that creators are, therefore, recognized and rewarded for their ingenuity and creativity.

WORLD METEOROLOGICAL ORGANIZATION (WMO)

The World Meteorological Organization coordinates global scientific research and data on the state and behaviour of the Earth's atmosphere, its interaction with the oceans, the climate it produces and the resulting distribution of water resources. WMO also provides vital information for early warnings of weather-, climate- and water-related phenomena, which cause nearly three quarters of all natural disasters, to save lives and minimize damage to property.

WORLD TOURISM ORGANIZATION (UNWTO)

The World Tourism Organization promotes the development of responsible, environmentally and socially friendly and universally accessible tourism. Tourism alone represents 5 per cent of the total economic activity and 6 to 7 per cent of the overall number of jobs worldwide. UNWTO is engaged in a global campaign to protect children from all forms of exploitation in tourism, including sexual exploitation, child labour and trafficking.

Funds and programmes

UNITED NATIONS CHILDREN'S FUND (UNICEF)

The United Nations Children's Fund is the main United Nations organization defending, promoting and protecting children's rights. It focuses especially on the world's most disadvantaged children. On the ground, UNICEF promotes education for all boys and girls, immunizes against common childhood diseases and provides other health services, water and nutrition to children and adolescents.

UNITED NATIONS CONFERENCE ON TRADE AND DEVELOPMENT (UNCTAD)

The United Nations Conference on Trade and Development promotes the integration of developing countries into the world economy. It helps shape debates and thinking on development and ensures that the policies of different countries and international action are mutually supportive in bringing about sustainable development.

UNITED NATIONS DEVELOPMENT PROGRAMME (UNDP)

The United Nations Development Programme is a global development network advocating for change and connecting countries to knowledge, experience and resources in order to help people build a better life. UNDP is on the ground in 177 countries, working with local inhabitants to find their own solutions to global and national development challenges.

UN-WOMEN, UNITED NATIONS ENTITY FOR GENDER EQUALITY AND THE EMPOWERMENT OF WOMEN

UN-Women, the United Nations Entity for Gender Equality and the Empowerment of Women seeks to eliminate discrimination against women and girls, to empower women and to achieve gender equality worldwide. In particular, UN-Women aims to uphold the human rights of girls, protecting them from all forms of violence and abuse and ensuring their access to health services and education.

UNITED NATIONS ENVIRONMENT (UNEP)

United Nations Environment is the leading global environmental authority that sets the global environmental agenda, promotes the coherent implementation of the environmental dimension of sustainable development within the United Nations system and serves as an authoritative advocate for the global environment.

OFFICE OF THE UNITED NATIONS HIGH COMMISSIONER FOR REFUGEES (UNHCR)

The Office of the United Nations High Commissioner for Refugees provides legal protection for displaced people and seeks long-lasting solutions to their problems by helping them either return voluntarily to their homes or settle in other countries. Nearly 50 per cent of the refugees worldwide are children. The UNHCR aims to uphold their rights, seeking to reunite them with their families and caregivers; protecting them from sexual exploitation, abuse, violence and military recruitment; and offering them education and training.

UNITED NATIONS HUMAN SETTLEMENTS PROGRAMME (UN-HABITAT)

The United Nations Human Settlements Programme is working towards a better urban future. Its mission is to promote socially and environmentally sustainable human settlements development and the achievement of adequate shelter for all.

UNITED NATIONS OFFICE ON DRUGS AND CRIME (UNODC)

The United Nations Office on Drugs and Crime focuses on organized crime and trafficking, building criminal justice systems, preventing illicit drug use and the spread of HIV among drug users and other vulnerable groups, ending corruption and preventing terrorism. Monitoring drug and crime trends and threats, it provides data that can help define drug and crime control priorities and help countries tackle these problems.

United Nations Population Fund (UNFPA)

The United Nations Population Fund promotes the right of women, men and children to enjoy a healthy life. The Fund supports countries in using population data to determine policies and programmes that help reduce poverty and ensure every pregnancy is wanted, every birth is safe and every girl and woman is treated with dignity and respect.

United Nations Relief and Works Agency for Palestine Refugees in the Near East (UNRWA)

The United Nations Relief and Works Agency for Palestine Refugees in the Near East provides assistance, protection and advocacy for registered Palestine refugees. It offers education, health care, relief and social services, camp infrastructure and improvement, community support, microfinance and emergency response, including in times of armed conflict.

World Food Programme (WFP)

The World Food Programme combats global hunger, which afflicts one out of every seven people on Earth. In emergencies, it is on the frontline, delivering food to save the lives of victims of war and natural disasters. After an emergency has passed, WFP uses food to help communities rebuild. Thanks to the school meals programmes, WFP directly affects the lives of millions of children, providing them with vital nourishment that in turn improves their health and boosts their attendance in school.

Research and training institutes

United Nations Institute for Disarmament Research (UNIDIR)

The United Nations Institute for Disarmament Research promotes research, creative thinking and dialogue on the disarmament and security challenges of today and tomorrow. The Institute deals with topics as diverse as nuclear materials, control of small arms ammunition, the security of refugee camps, disarmament as humanitarian action, peacekeeping and remote sensing technologies in the service of peace.

United Nations Institute for Training and Research (UNITAR)

The United Nations Institute for Training and Research carries out research and training activities and develops pedagogical materials. Often working with other academic institutions, it offers instruction in the fields of peace and security, human rights, social and economic development, the environment, multilateral diplomacy and international cooperation.

United Nations Interregional Crime and Justice Research Institute (UNICRI)

The United Nations Interregional Crime and Justice Research Institute tackles the threat of crimes to peace, development and political stability. Its goals are to advance an understanding of crime-related problems, to foster fair and efficient criminal justice systems, including juvenile justice, to support the respect of international instruments of justice and other standards and to facilitate international law enforcement cooperation and judicial assistance.

United Nations Research Institute for Social Development (UNRISD)

The mission of the United Nations Research Institute for Social Development is to generate knowledge and articulate policy alternatives on contemporary development issues, thereby contributing to the broader goals of the United Nations system of reducing poverty and inequality, advancing well-being and human rights, and creating more democratic and just societies. The Institute was established as an autonomous space within the United Nations system for the conduct of policy-relevant, cutting-edge research on social development that is pertinent to the work of the United Nations Secretariat, specialized agencies and national institutions.

United Nations System Staff College (UNSSC)

The United Nations System Staff College runs courses for United Nations personnel, assisting the staff of United Nations organizations in developing the skills and competencies needed to meet today's global challenges.

United Nations University (UNU)

The United Nations University contributes to the advancement of knowledge in fields relevant to the United Nations and to the application of that knowledge in formulating sound principles, policies, strategies and programmes for action. Its activities are focused on five interlinked, interdependent thematic clusters: peace, security and human rights; human and socio-economic development and good governance; global health, population and sustainable livelihoods; global change and sustainable development, and science, technology, innovation and society.

Other entities

Joint United Nations Programme on HIV/AIDS (UNAIDS)

The Joint United Nations Programme on HIV/AIDS is an innovative partnership that garners support for achieving complete access for all to HIV prevention, treatment, care and support. The objective is zero new HIV infections, zero discrimination and zero AIDS-related deaths. Since this mandate requires long-term investment, the strategy is to bolster prevention, treatment, care and support, as well as human rights and gender equality for all those who are affected.

United Nations Office for Disaster Risk Reduction (UNISDR)

The United Nations Office for Disaster Risk Reduction (UNISDR) was established to facilitate the implementation of the International Strategy for Disaster Reduction (ISDR). It was created to be the focal point in the United Nations system for the coordination of disaster risk reduction, and ensures synergies among the relevant activities of United Nations agencies and regional organizations, and related activities in socio-economic and humanitarian fields. It aims to build resilient nations and communities, an essential condition for sustainable development.

United Nations Office for Project Services (UNOPS)

The United Nations Office for Project Services aims to expand the capacity of the United Nations System and its partners to implement peacebuilding, humanitarian and development operations that matter for people in need. Core services include human resources and financial management as well as the procurement of material and other services.

Related organizations

INTERNATIONAL ATOMIC ENERGY AGENCY (IAEA)

The International Atomic Energy Agency serves as the global focal point for nuclear cooperation. It assists countries in planning for and using nuclear science and technology for peaceful purposes, such as the generation of electricity, and it develops nuclear safety standards. IAEA also uses a system of inspections to ensure that States comply with their commitment to use nuclear material and facilities only for peaceful purposes.

ORGANIZATION FOR THE PROHIBITION OF CHEMICAL WEAPONS (OPCW)

The Organization for the Prohibition of Chemical Weapons is dedicated to the implementation of the Convention on the Prohibition of the Development, Production, Stockpiling and Use of Chemical Weapons and on their Destruction. The main obligation under the Convention is the prohibition of use and production of chemical weapons, as well as the destruction of all chemical weapons. The destruction activities are verified by the OPCW which also verifies that toxic chemicals that States produce are not intended for use as weapons of mass destruction.

PREPARATORY COMMISSION FOR THE COMPREHENSIVE NUCLEAR-TEST-BAN TREATY ORGANIZATION (CTBTO)

The Preparatory Commission for the Comprehensive Nuclear-Test-Ban Treaty Organization promotes the Comprehensive Nuclear-Test-Ban Treaty, which prohibits nuclear explosions by anyone anywhere on the Earth's surface, in the atmosphere, underwater or underground. CTBTO also has a monitoring system set up around the world to make sure that no nuclear explosion goes undetected. The Treaty will enter into force when the required number of countries ratifies it.

WORLD TRADE ORGANIZATION (WTO)

The World Trade Organization is a forum for governments to negotiate trade agreements and settle trade disputes. It operates a system of trade rules. WTO is the place where Member States try to sort out the trade problems they face with each other.

MESSENGERS OF PEACE AND GOODWILL AMBASSADORS

The United Nations Messengers of Peace and Goodwill Ambassadors help focus attention on the work of the United Nations.

From the earliest days of the United Nations, actors, artists, sportsmen and women, gymnasts, designers, musicians, ballet dancers, astronauts, entrepreneurs, scientists, writers, philosophers, fashion models and members of governments and royal families—talented and compassionate women and men from around the world—have lent their names, public recognition and fame in support of the United Nations' work for a better world.

While Goodwill and Honorary Ambassadors mainly promote the work of the United Nations agencies they represent, the Messengers of Peace champion the work of the United Nations in general and are appointed directly by the Secretary-General.

The Messengers of Peace are initially chosen for a period of two years, although some of the Messengers have served for much longer.

HRH
Princess Haya

Daniel
Barenboim

Paulo
Coelho

Leonardo
DiCaprio

Michael
Douglas

Jane
Goodall

Lang
Lang

Yo-Yo
Ma

Midori
Gotō

Edward
Norton

Charlize
Theron

Stevie
Wonder

Malala
Yousafzai

Chapter 3

ECONOMIC AND SOCIAL DEVELOPMENT

QUICK FACTS ON ECONOMIC AND SOCIAL DEVELOPMENT

- The international poverty line is currently defined as 1.90 US dollars per person per day. Today, an estimated 767 million people live in **extreme poverty**, down from 1.7 billion people in 1999. Still, in 2017, the United Nations helped improve the livelihoods of more than 1 billion people.

- In 2016, an estimated 155 million children under age 5 were stunted (low height for their age), down from 198 million in 2000. Globally, the **stunting rate** fell from 32.7 per cent in 2000 to 22.9 per cent in 2016. Southern Asia and sub-Saharan Africa accounted for three quarters of children under age 5 with stunted growth in 2016.

- The United Nations helps 30 million women survive pregnancy and childbirth. In 2015, an estimated 303,000 women worldwide died during pregnancy and childbirth. This translates into a **global maternal mortality** ratio of 216 deaths per 100,000 live births in 2015, a 37 per cent reduction since 2000. Achieving the United Nations global target of less than 70 maternal deaths per 100,000 live births by 2030 will require more than doubling that rate.

- About 263 million children and adolescents were **out of school** in 2014. Of these, 61 million were children of primary-school age, 60 million were adolescents of lower-secondary-school age, and 142 million were teens of upper-secondary-school age. They largely resided in sub-Saharan Africa and Southern Asia, where educational systems struggle to keep up with population growth.

- Physical and sexual **violence against women and girls** exist in all regions, and much of it is at the hands of intimate partners. Between 2005 and 2016 a survey found that in 87 countries (including 30 from developed regions), 19 per cent of girls and women aged 15-49 had experienced physical and/or sexual violence by an intimate partner.

- Currently, more than 2 billion people are affected by **water stress**, which will only increase with population growth and the effects of climate change. Achieving universal access to drinking water, sanitation and hygiene and ensuring that services are safely managed remain major challenges.

- The landmark Paris Agreement brings nations together to strengthen the response to **climate change**. It aims to keep the global temperature rise this century to below 2 degrees Celsius above pre-industrial levels and as close as possible to 1.5 degrees, while building countries' resilience to the adverse effects of climate change. The Agreement entered into force on 4 November 2016.

- About 10 million hectares of farmland are lost every year due to **ecosystem degradation** while deforestation and acidification of the oceans continue to increase.

- By 2015, an estimated 880 million urban residents lived in slums, compared to 792 million in 2000. Substandard **living conditions** and the lack of basic services hit children and young people the hardest, diminishing their prospects for good health and education.

DEVELOPMENT: A PRIORITY FOR THE UNITED NATIONS

Although people generally associate the United Nations with issues of peace and security, a large portion of the Organization's resources is in fact devoted to advancing the Charter's pledge to "promote higher standards of living, full employment, and conditions of economic and social progress and development". The United Nations is guided in its endeavours by the conviction that lasting international peace and security are possible only if the economic and social well-being of people everywhere is assured.

Poverty and development

Development implies that the quality of life for individuals, families and communities is improving, which in turn allows people to become more productive. Increased productivity places a country in a better position to trade with other countries, and more trade means more goods and services to continue improving the living conditions of more people.

Development is a complex process, though. Reaching an acceptable standard of living for all includes giving everyone access to the basics: food, housing, jobs, health services, education, safety and security. A country must concurrently pay attention to social, economic, political, cultural and environmental issues to ensure that development is sustainable and beneficial to all.[1]

Development is also a human right, as per the Declaration on the Right to Development of 1986. You will find more information on this in chapter five.

Globalization

Globalization is not new. People have been travelling to other parts of the world and trading goods and services for millennia. This process brings the world

FOCUS ON

What poverty means

- Poverty is more than a lack of money. It is a pronounced deprivation of well-being.

- Poverty means having insufficient food and basic nutrition, limited or non-existent access to health services and education, a lack of freedom and representation.

- Poverty is also a fear of tomorrow, allowing people to only think about living one day at a time.

- Poverty means marginalization. Poor people are often treated as invisible, voiceless and powerless to improve their living conditions.

---

[1]   See World Bank, "Issues: Development," available from http://youthink.worldbank.org/issues/development

A UNDP project helped empower herder groups in Mongolia, improving their livelihood while protecting the biodiversity of the region. ■ UN PHOTO/ESKINDER DEBEBE

closer through the exchange of products, information, knowledge and culture. Over the last few decades, though, the integration of economies and societies around the world has happened at a much faster and more dramatic pace because of unprecedented advancements in technology, communications, science, transport and industry.[2]

While globalization is a catalyst for and a consequence of human progress, it is also a difficult process that creates significant challenges and problems and therefore requires adjustments. Many people have criticized the effects of globalization, stressing that inequalities in the current global trading system hurt some countries more than others, some people more than others and some job sectors more than others. They say that the process has exploited people in developing countries at the expense of jobs in the developed world, caused massive disruptions and produced only a few benefits for too few people at the top of the social pyramid.

For all countries to be able to reap the benefits of globalization, the international community must continue working to reduce distortions in international trade (for instance, cutting agricultural subsidies and trade barriers) that favour developed countries, in order to create a fairer system for everybody.

[2]   Ibid.

United Nations action

Issues such as refugee population flows, organized crime, terrorism, corruption, drug trafficking, AIDS and other epidemics and, of course, climate change, are not limited to one country in isolation. They are global challenges requiring coordinated international action. Due to migration, social disruption and conflict, the impact of persistent poverty and unemployment in one region can quickly be felt in others.

Similarly, in the age of a global economy, financial instability in one country is instantly felt in the markets of others. There is also a growing consensus on the role played by democracy, human rights, popular participation, good governance and the empowerment of women in fostering economic and social development. This awakening has been exemplified and illustrated in a dramatic manner by the unrest that has rocked the Middle East and North Africa since 2011 and shows no sign of abating.

Obstacles and challenges to development know no borders. With its 193 Member States, the United Nations provides a platform for discussion and formulation of developmental policies. To focus attention on certain issues, the United Nations organizes global conferences and promotes international development days, years and decades. As the global centre for consensus building, the United Nations set priorities for international cooperation, such as the **Millennium Development Goals (MDGs)** which were followed by the **Sustainable Development Goals (SDGs),** to assist countries in their efforts and to foster a supportive environment. United Nations development efforts have profoundly affected the lives and well-being of millions of people throughout the world.

At the **United Nations Millennium Summit** held in September 2000 in New York, 189 world leaders endorsed the *Millennium Declaration*, which was translated

DID YOU KNOW?

Investing in women helps eradicate poverty faster

Women perform 66 per cent of the world's work and produce 50 per cent of the food, but they earn only 10 per cent of the income and own just 1 per cent of the property.

When girls are able to obtain a secondary education, a country's economy grows through women's increased participation in the labour force and their productivity and earnings. When an educated girl earns an income, she reinvests 90 per cent of it in her family—an extremely high number compared to boys, who devote 35 per cent of their income to their families.

Education and work give women increased influence and power to make decisions in the household. Maternal health and children's education and nutrition are all dependent upon how well limited resources are accessed, allocated and used.

FROM THE MDGs TO THE SDGs

The United Nations Millennium Development Goals (2000-2015),
and the Sustainable Development Goals (2016–2030)

into a road map setting out eight time-bound goals to be reached by 2015, known as the Millennium Development Goals (MDGs).

The MDGs, ranging from halving extreme poverty to halting the spread of HIV/AIDS and providing universal primary education, served as a framework for collective action and galvanized unprecedented efforts to meet the needs of the world's poorest people.

SUSTAINABLE DEVELOPMENT GOALS

On 1 January 2016, the Sustainable Development Goals (SDGs) of the *2030 Agenda for Sustainable Development*, adopted by world leaders in September 2015 at the historic United Nations Sustainable Development Summit, officially came into force.

The SDGs, also known as Global Goals, build on the success of the MDGs and aim to go further by addressing the root causes of poverty and the universal need for development that works for all people. The 17 goals with 169 targets cover the three dimensions of sustainable development: economic growth, social inclusion and environmental protection.

Whereas the MDGs were intended for action in developing countries only, the SDGs are universal and apply to all. Countries will mobilize efforts to end all forms of poverty, fight inequalities and tackle climate change, while ensuring that no one is left behind.

The 17 goals

GOAL 1
End poverty in all its forms everywhere

Extreme poverty rates have been cut by more than half since 1990, yet one in five people in developing regions still live on less than $1.90 a day. Poverty is more than the lack of income and resources to ensure a sustainable livelihood. Its manifestations also include hunger and malnutrition, social discrimination, limited access to basic services such as education, shelter and medical care, and lack of participation in decision-making. Ending poverty means providing all men and women with equal access to economic resources, basic services, property, natural resources, new technology and financial services. It also means building resilience of the poor and the vulnerable to reduce their exposure and vulnerability to climate-related extreme events and other economic, social and environmental shocks and disasters.

GOAL 2
End hunger, achieve food security and improved nutrition and promote sustainable agriculture

Making sure that every woman, man child and infant have safe, nutritious and sufficient food lies at the heart of goal 2. To nourish today's 795 million hungry and the additional 2 billion people expected by 2050, a profound change of the global food and agricultural system is needed. This goal focuses on developing sustainable food production systems and resilient agricultural practices that can increase productivity, maintain ecosystems and adapt to climate change.

In Senegal, the United Nations provided these women with a diesel engine powering a variety of equipment, so they no longer spend their days gathering firewood. Instead, they now sell the mango and sweet potato jam they produce, allowing them to earn much-needed income. ■ UN PHOTO/EVAN SCHNEIDER

Its key targets include supporting small-scale food producers; regulating world agricultural and food commodity markets; and investing in rural infrastructure, research and technology development in developing countries. If properly conducted, agriculture, forestry and fisheries can provide nutritious food for all and generate decent incomes, while supporting people-centred rural development and protecting the environment.

GOAL 3
Ensure healthy lives and promote well-being for all at all ages

 Societies prosper when all people are in good health, have access to medical care and know how to take decisions to stay healthy throughout their lives. Goal 3 aims to further reduce maternal mortality and preventable deaths of infants and children, and end communicable diseases such as HIV, malaria and tuberculosis. It calls for real progress in achieving universal health coverage, universal access to sexual and reproductive health care services as well as safe, affordable and effective medicines and vaccines for all. This goal is also about preventing and treating substance abuse, halving the deaths and injuries from traffic accidents, and reducing non-communicable and environmental diseases.

GOAL 4
Ensure inclusive and equitable quality education for all and promote lifelong learning opportunities for all

 Education can help lift people out of poverty, provide better opportunities and contribute to the promotion of sustainable development, human rights and peace. Every girl, boy, woman and man should be given equal access to quality education of all levels as well as technical, vocational and tertiary training needed for employment, decent jobs and entrepreneurship. Extra efforts are required to eliminate gender disparities and ensure that the disadvantaged, including persons with disabilities, indigenous people and children in vulnerable situations, receive quality education. This goal also seeks to provide safe and inclusive learning environments for all, and increase the numbers of scholarships and qualified teachers for developing countries, especially the least developed countries and small island developing States.

GOAL 5
Achieve gender equality and empower all women and girls

 Gender equality is not only a fundamental human right but also a necessary foundation for a peaceful, prosperous and sustainable world. Goal 5 calls for accelerated action to end all forms of discrimination and violence against women and girls, including trafficking, forced marriage and female genital mutilation, and to protect their sexual, reproductive health and reproductive rights. Providing women and girls with equal access to education, health care, technology, decent work and leadership opportunities at all levels of political, economic and public life will fuel sustainable economies and benefit societies and humanity at large. UNiTE to End Violence against Women, Every Woman Every Child and HeForShe are a few of the global movements led by the United Nations to raise awareness and mobilize support for achieving gender equality.

GOAL 6
Ensure availability and sustainable management of water and sanitation for all

Clean, accessible water is essential for life. Water scarcity, poor water quality and inadequate sanitation negatively impact the food security, livelihood and educational opportunities of billions. Goal 6 was conceived to achieve universal and equitable access to safe and affordable drinking water, sanitation and hygiene for all, and to end open defecation. It underscores the need to reduce pollution, improve water-use efficiency and waste management. Some other key targets are to protect and restore water-related ecosystems; help local communities manage their water supply; and encourage countries to work together for the common good in areas with transboundary water sources.

GOAL 7
Ensure access to affordable, reliable, sustainable and modern energy for all

Energy is central to nearly every major challenge and opportunity the world faces today, such as jobs, security, climate change and food production. Goal 7 was created to ensure universal access to affordable, reliable and modern energy. It requires a rapid increase in energy efficiency, and the share of renewable energy in the global energy mix. International cooperation needs to be enhanced to support and expand the supply of modern forms of energy to developing countries, and to facilitate clean energy research and technology. The United Nations's Sustainable Energy for All (SE4ALL) initiative empowers leaders to broker partnerships and unlock finance to achieve universal access to sustainable energy.

GOAL 8
Promote sustained, inclusive and sustainable economic growth, full and productive employment and decent work for all

Sustainable economic growth requires societies to create the conditions that allow people to have quality jobs that stimulate the economy while protecting the environment. Goal 8 focuses on achieving full and productive employment, safe and secure working environments and equal pay for all women and men, including youth and persons with disabilities. Immediate and effective measures must be taken to end forced labour, modern slavery, human trafficking and child labour. Higher levels of economic productivity can be achieved through diversification, technological upgrading and innovation. This goal encourages entrepreneurship, particularly the growth of micro-, small- and medium-sized enterprises. Sustainable tourism is an example of bringing together public and private sector decision-makers and the public to create jobs and promote local culture and products.

GOAL 9
Build resilient infrastructure, promote inclusive and sustainable industrialization and foster innovation

 Reliable and resilient infrastructure like transport, energy, water and information and communication technology (ICT) is crucial for economic development and human well-being, especially in developing countries. The growth of new industries generates income, employment and can significantly improve the living standard for many. Goal 9 aims to upgrade infrastructure and retrofit industries to make them sustainable, with increased resource-use efficiency and greater adoption of environmentally sound technologies. Technological progress is the foundation for such changes. The goal supports scientific research and innovation in all countries, and particularly seeks to provide universal and affordable access to ICT and the Internet in order to bridge the digital divide.

GOAL 10
Reduce inequality within and among countries

 Goal 10 supports disadvantaged and marginalized populations by fighting inequalities within and among countries. It calls for social, economic and political inclusion of all, irrespective of age, sex, disability, race, ethnicity, origin, religion or economic or other status. At the international level, inequality can be tackled by enhancing the representation and voice for developing countries in decision-making, regulating the global financial market, and encouraging official development assistance to States where the need is greatest. This goal also aims to facilitate orderly, safe, regular and responsible migration and mobility of people, and to reduce the transaction costs of migrant remittances.

GOAL 11
Make cities and human settlements inclusive, safe, resilient and sustainable

 By 2030, almost 60 per cent of the world's population will live in urban areas. Cities are hubs for ideas, commerce, culture, science, productivity, social development and much more. Goal 11 was created to ensure access to safe and affordable housing, basic services, upgraded slums and sustainable transport systems for all. It seeks to promote green public spaces and reduce the environmental impact of cities, with special attention to air quality and waste management. To prevent deaths and economic losses caused by disasters, the goal calls on the world's cities to adopt policies and plans towards resource efficiency, mitigation and adaptation to climate change, and implement holistic disaster risk management at all levels in line with the Sendai Framework for Disaster Risk Reduction 2015-2030.

In October 2016, the New Urban Agenda was adopted in Quito, Ecuador, during the United Nations Conference on Housing and Sustainable Urban Development, to set global standards for achieving sustainable urban development.

GOAL 12
Ensure sustainable consumption and production patterns

Sustainable consumption and production is about reducing the environmental and social costs of economic activities. Its implementation requires a systematic approach among all actors in the supply chain of products and services. Businesses or producers should be encouraged to adopt sustainable practices and reduce their use of resources, while costumers can be engaged through awareness-raising and education on sustainable lifestyles. Every year one third of all food produced globally goes to waste. This has to be stopped at both retail and customer levels. It is possible to significantly reduce the generation of waste through prevention, recycling and reuse. Environmentally sound management of chemicals and all waste should be implemented throughout their life cycle to minimize their impact on human health and the environment.

GOAL 13
Take urgent action to combat climate change and its impacts

Climate change is affecting every country on every continent. Its impacts include changing weather patterns, rising sea level and extreme weather events. Greenhouse gas emissions from human activities are now at their highest levels in history. Goal 13 is a call for immediate action by all countries to lower greenhouse gas emissions, build resilience and improve education on climate change. Affordable, scalable solutions such as renewable energy and clean technologies are available to enable countries to leapfrog to greener, more resilient economies. Because climate change is a global challenge with no respect for national borders, the implementation of this goal requires that developed countries fulfil their commitment to mobilize funds and support capacity-building for developing countries, in particular the least developed countries and small island developing States.

In December 2015, the Paris Agreement was adopted at the United Nations Climate Change Conference (COP21) in Paris. In the Agreement, which opened for signature in April and entered into force on 4 November 2016, all countries agreed to work to limit global temperature rise to below 2 degrees Celsius, and to strive for 1.5 degrees Celsius.

GOAL 14
Conserve and sustainably use the oceans, seas and marine resources for sustainable development

 Oceans play an essential role in human well-being and social and economic development worldwide. Over 3 billion people depend on marine and coastal biodiversity for their livelihoods. Goal 14 focuses on the sustainable management and protection of marine and coastal ecosystems. Its key targets include preventing and significantly reducing marine pollution; minimizing ocean acidification; increasing the economic benefits of small island developing States and the least developed countries; ending overfishing and illegal fishing to restore fish stocks; and developing marine science and research capacity. This goal also draws attention to the role of international law in the protection of oceans and their resources, as specified in the United Nations Convention on the Law of the Sea.

The Ocean Conference, convened on 5-9 June 2017 in New York, was the first major United Nations conference focusing on ocean sustainability and the implementation of goal 14.

GOAL 15
Protect, restore and promote sustainable use of terrestrial ecosystems, sustainably manage forests, combat desertification, halt and reverse land degradation and halt biodiversity loss

 Forests cover 30 per cent of the Earth's surface. Around 1.6 billion people depend on forests for their livelihood. This includes 70 million indigenous people. Goal 15 aims to ensure the conservation, restoration and sustainable use of terrestrial and inland freshwater ecosystems, in particular forests, wetlands, mountains and drylands. It seeks to sustainably manage forests, combat desertification and restore degraded land. Urgent action is needed to halt the loss of biodiversity, and to protect the threatened species from wildlife crimes such as poaching and trafficking. This goal urges all countries to integrate the conservation and sustainable use of biodiversity and ecosystems into their development plans, and mobilize financing from all sources to achieve these targets.

GOAL 16
Promote peaceful and inclusive societies for sustainable development, provide access to justice for all and build effective, accountable and inclusive institutions at all levels

 Goal 16 sets out to significantly reduce all forms of violence and crimes that threaten the foundation of peace, including abuse, exploitation, trafficking and illicit financial and arms flows as well as discriminatory laws and practices. Everyone should have equal access to justice, legal identity and fundamental freedoms, and be supported by effective, accountable and transparent institutions. Successful implementation of this goal requires lasting solutions to fight corruption, pro-

mote rule of law and ensure inclusive decision-making. At the international level, the goal pledges support for strengthening national institutions in developing countries and broadening their participation in global governance.

GOAL 17
Strengthen the means of implementation and revitalize the Global Partnership for Sustainable Development

 A successful sustainable development agenda requires partnerships at all levels between governments, the private sector
and civil society. Urgent action is required to mobilize, redi-
rect and unlock the transformative power of private resources.
Long-term investments, including foreign direct investment, are
needed in critical sectors such as sustainable energy, infrastructure, transport and communications technologies. The public sector must set a clear di-
rection and retool review and monitoring frameworks, regulations and incen-
tive structures to enable such investments. National oversight mechanisms
such as supreme audit institutions and oversight functions by legislatures
should be strengthened. This goal underscores the need to enhance North-
South, South-South and triangular regional and international cooperation, and
calls on developed countries to provide assistance to developing countries in
areas of financing, technology, capacity-building, and promotion of an open,
non-discriminatory multilateral trading system.

DEVELOPMENT FOR TODAY AND TOMORROW

Sustainable development

What is sustainable development?

The world's population of 7.4 billion is likely to increase to 11.2 billion by 2100.
The demand for diminishing natural resources is growing. Income gaps are
widening. Sustainable development calls for a decent standard of living for
everyone today without compromising the needs of future generations. In other words, we must use our resources wisely.

Sustainable development requires us to conserve more and waste less. In
industrialized nations, many people live beyond nature's means. For example, one person in a very rich country uses as much energy as 80 people in
a very poor country. Overconsumption leads to waste, which pollutes our
environment and uses up our resources.

Crushing poverty and growing populations also put great pressure on the
environment. When land and forests, which provide food, natural resources
and employment, are exhausted, people find it harder—sometimes impossi-
ble—to survive. Many go to cities, crowding into unhealthy and unsafe slums.

If poor people are forced to destroy their local environments to survive, many
generations of people in all countries will suffer the consequences.

Exhibition by artist Mona Sfeir: Human life has a huge impact on the environment as visible and invisible waste pollutes the globe, affecting ecosystems and bringing diseases to—or even causing the deaths of—humans, animals and plants. ■ UN PHOTO/JEAN-MARC FERRÉ

Does sustainable development work?

Over the last three decades, there have been many examples of successful sustainable development in the fields of energy, agriculture, urban planning, and production and consumption:

- ■ In the United States in 2016, scientists in Tennessee are changing the way Americans do laundry—using vibrations instead of heat to dry their clothes. This new technology is expected to dry clothes in half the time and use 70 per cent less energy than today's products.

- ■ In Kenya, innovative finance mechanisms have stimulated new investments in renewable energy sources, including solar, wind, small hydro, biogas and municipal waste energy, generating income and employment.

- ■ In China, steps to shift to a low-carbon growth strategy based on the development of renewable energy sources have created jobs, income and revenue streams for promising low-carbon industries.

- ■ In Uganda, a transition to organic agriculture has generated revenue and income for smallholder farmers and benefited the economy, society and environment.

- In Nepal, community forestry, led by local groups, contributed to restoring forest resources after a steady decline in the 1990s.

- In Canada, EcoLogo—one of North America's most respected environmental certification marks—has promoted thousands of products that meet rigorous environmental standards.

- In France, in 2015, renewable energy production increased by more than 23% (not including hydroelectricity) and 2,000 jobs were created in 2014 in the wind-energy sector.

- In 2017, many countries announced that vehicles using fossil fuels would be phased out and banned over the next two decades. This was the case of France, Germany and the United Kingdom for example.

The United Nations and climate change

The **United Nations Framework Convention on Climate Change** (**UNFCCC**) is an international treaty that was adopted on 9 May 1992, and opened for signature at the Earth Summit in Rio de Janeiro in June of the same year. It entered into force on 21 March 1994, after a sufficient number of countries had ratified it. In 2017, there were 197 ratifications.

The UNFCCC objective is to "stabilize greenhouse gas concentrations in the atmosphere at a level that would prevent dangerous anthropogenic interference with our climate system. The framework sets no binding limits on greenhouse gas emissions for individual countries and contains no enforcement mechanisms. Instead, the framework outlines how specific international treaties (called "protocols" or "agreements") may be negotiated to specify further action towards the objective of the UNFCCC. The Convention enjoys broad legitimacy, largely due to its nearly universal membership.

The parties to the convention have met annually from 1995 in Conferences of the Parties (COP) to assess progress in dealing with climate change. In 1997, the **Kyoto Protocol** was concluded and established legally binding obligations for developed countries to reduce their greenhouse gas emissions. In 2015, the **Paris Agreement** was adopted, governing emission reductions from 2020 on through commitments of countries in ambitious Nationally Determined Contributions. It entered into force on 4 November 2016.

Linking environment and development

The environment is everything that surrounds us. It is the air we breathe, the water we drink, the soil in which we grow our food, and all living beings. Development is what we do with these resources to improve our lives.

We change the world—literally

All over the world we do things that we think will make our lives better, but we forget that everything we do changes us and our environment. Sometimes we

Climate change: The Paris Agreement

The Paris Agreement builds upon the **United Nations Framework Convention on Climate Change (UNFCCC)** and—for the first time—brings all nations into a common cause to undertake ambitious efforts to combat climate change and adapt to its effects, with enhanced support to assist developing countries to do so. As such, it charts a new course in the global climate effort.

The Paris Agreement's central aim is to strengthen the global response to the threat of climate change by keeping a global temperature rise this century below 2 degrees Celsius above pre-industrial levels and to pursue efforts to limit the temperature increase even further to 1.5 degrees Celsius. Additionally, the agreement aims to strengthen the ability of countries to deal with the impacts of climate change. To reach these ambitious goals, appropriate financial flows, a new technology framework and an enhanced capacity-building framework is being put in place, thus supporting action by developing countries and the most vulnerable countries in line with their own national objectives. The Agreement also provides for enhanced transparency of action and support through a robust transparency framework.

The Paris Agreement requires all Parties to put forward their best efforts through "nationally determined contributions" and to strengthen these efforts in the years ahead. This includes requirements that countries report regularly on their emissions and on their implementation efforts.

Assessments will be carried out every five years on the collective progress towards achieving the purpose of the Agreement and to inform further individual actions by Parties.

don't see how connected we are to the Earth and to each other, but the connections are there:

- Medicines that save lives in Germany may depend on plants that grow in the forests of Costa Rica.

- Pollution from automobiles in London or Mexico City may affect the climate in Rabat or Tokyo.

- Carbon dioxide and other gases from factories and cars cause the atmosphere to heat up. This rise in temperature is changing the world's climate.

- Forests help free the air of carbon dioxide, but many forests are being cut down for their wood or to clear land for farms.

The natural world around us is a fragile place that requires care, respect and knowledge. Air pollution, waterborne diseases, toxic chemicals and natural disasters are just some of the environmental challenges that humankind faces.

Protecting the environment

The United Nations plays a key role in shaping international action to protect our environment, with United Nations Environment (UNEP) leading these global efforts. The United Nations conducts research, monitors the state of the environment and advises governments on ways to preserve their natural resources. Most importantly, it brings governments together to make international laws to solve particular environmental problems.

Here are some important results of action by the United Nations in addition to the UNFCCC, the Kyoto Protocol and the Paris Agreement:

- The Declaration and Programme of Action for the Sustainable Development of Small Island Developing States (1994) calls on countries to take special action to promote the social and economic development of 40 small island developing States. Many of these States have very limited resources and have been unable to reap the benefits of globalization.

- The Convention to Combat Desertification (1994) seeks to resolve problems of overcultivation, deforestation, overgrazing and poor irrigation. One quarter of the Earth's land is threatened by desertification. The livelihoods of over one billion people in more than 100 countries are jeopardized, as farming and grazing land become less productive.

- The United Nations Convention on Biological Diversity (1992) seeks to protect and conserve the wide variety of animal and plant life that is vital for human survival.

Water for life

Water is absolutely essential for life. No living being on the planet can survive without it. It is a prerequisite for human health and well-being as well as for the preservation of the environment.

SAFE WATER?

- Globally, 663 million people still do not have access to safe drinking water, which means that more than one in 10 people were without access in 2017.

- Every year millions of people, most of them children, die from diseases associated with inadequate water supply, sanitation and hygiene.

- Water scarcity, poor water quality and inadequate sanitation negatively impact food security, livelihood choices and educational opportunities for poor families across the world.

Women and girls are overwhelmingly the water haulers of the world.
This task consumes valuable time and energy, which they could otherwise devote to different
types of productive work, childcare and education. ■ UN PHOTO/ALBERT GONGÁLEZ-FARRÁN

- Water-related natural disasters such as floods, tropical storms and tsunamis exact a heavy toll in human life and suffering.

All too regularly, drought afflicts some of the world's poorest countries, exacerbating hunger and malnutrition.

WATER AND DEVELOPMENT

Beyond meeting basic human needs, water is a valuable resource. Water supply and sanitation services are critical to sustainable development:

- Water is a major source of energy in some parts of the world, while in others its potential to provide energy remains largely untapped.

- Water is necessary for agriculture and many industrial processes.

- In many countries water provides an integral part of transport systems.

Water challenges will increase significantly in the coming years. Population growth and rising incomes will lead to greater water consumption, as well as more waste. Urban populations in developing countries will grow dramatically, generating demand well beyond the capacity of already inadequate water supply and sanitation infrastructures and services. By 2050, at least one in four people will live in a country affected by chronic or recurring shortages of fresh water.

The importance of biodiversity

BIODIVERSITY AND POVERTY

Biological diversity is at the core of the world's efforts to alleviate poverty. For millennia, humankind has used the Earth's ecosystem to maintain its well-being and fuel economic development. In addition, many belief systems, worldviews and identities centre around biodiversity. Yet despite its fundamental importance, biodiversity continues to be lost at an alarming rate.

Healthy ecosystems provide a variety of goods and services, among them food, medicine, soil formation, air quality, water supply and the cultural and aesthetic value of certain plants and animal species. Protection and proper management of biologically diverse resources is essential to all aspects of sustainable development, especially to the agriculture, livestock, forestry, fishing and tourism sectors.

BIODIVERSITY AND DEVELOPMENT

Today, more than 1.6 billion people depend on biodiversity and basic ecosystem goods and services for their livelihoods. Development does not stop at poverty reduction; environmental sustainability is essential for the achievement of the Sustainable Development Goals and the elimination of poverty.

Biodiversity and development are closely linked: biodiversity sustains development, and development impacts biodiversity, either positively or negatively. Although biodiversity does not contribute directly to all sectors of development, sustainable growth cannot be achieved if biodiversity is compromised by development efforts.

Since the poor are particularly dependent on the goods and services supplied by the planet, development strategies that fail to prioritize biodiversity undermine poverty alleviation and are therefore counterproductive.

The United Nations adopted the Strategic Plan for Biodiversity aimed at inspiring broad-based action in support of biodiversity over the present decade. The General Assembly also declared 2011-2020 the United Nations Decade for Biodiversity.

QUICK FACTS ON INTERNATIONAL PEACE AND SECURITY

- Since 1948, there have been **71 United Nations-led peacekeeping operations**. In 2017, the United Nations had 16 ongoing peacekeeping operations around the world.

- Approximately 112,300 soldiers, police officers, volunteers and civilian personnel serve in United Nations **peacekeeping operations** around the world today, providing essential security and support to millions of people on four continents.

- The United Nations has helped broker over 170 **peace settlements** since its creation.

- Sustainable Development Goal 16 focuses on promotion of **peaceful societies**, provision for access to justice for all and building accountable institutions at all levels.

- United Nations **peacebuilding** in post-conflict areas often includes overseeing the collection and destruction of hundreds of thousands of weapons and facilitating the reintegration of former combatants into civil society.

- The United Nations played a crucial role in encouraging countries to support the 1997 Ottawa Convention, which advocates a total ban on the production, export and use of **landmines**. The Organization continues to promote universal adherence to this treaty today.

- United Nations support has resulted in a wide range of peace and security agreements, including the Nuclear Non-Proliferation Treaty, the Comprehensive Nuclear-Test-Ban Treaty and treaties to establish **nuclear-free zones**.

- Five countries recorded the majority of **terrorist attacks** in 2015-2016: Iraq, Nigeria, Afghanistan, Pakistan and Syria.

- Most violent conflicts today are fought within States, primarily with **small arms and light weapons**. Up to 8 million small arms are produced every year, and their use accounts for 60 to 90 per cent of direct conflict deaths.

- The approved budget for United Nations Peacekeeping Operations is $6.8 billion for the year of July 2017-June 2018, which is less than 0.5 per cent of **global military expenditures**.

Conflict—whether neighbourhood crime and violence, civil war, or war between two or more countries—is often both a cause and consequence of poverty. Research shows that the combination of poverty, economic decline and dependence on exporting natural resources drives conflict across all regions. Escaping this "conflict trap" remains an elusive goal for many recovering countries: an estimated 40 per cent of which relapse into violence within 10 years.

Conflict is expensive and affects everyone. Within a country, the cost of war continues long after the fighting ends:

- **Deaths**: Combatants make up only a small fraction of overall deaths, injuries and misery. Declining or non-existent health services can lead to more people dying, including non-combatants. About half the deaths resulting from a conflict happen after peace is declared.

- **Flight and disease**: Numerous people flee combat. Refugees often pick up diseases as they escape and spread them across borders as they seek sanctuary.

- **Lost childhoods**: Generations of children and young people miss out on a stable home, childhood and school. Often, they are recruited as soldiers. Once the war ends, it is challenging for these young people to readapt to normal life and think of leading their countries into the future.

- **Landmines**: Mines left in battlefields put land out of use for years, making it difficult for farmers to produce food. Many countries find it too expensive to locate and remove landmines.

- **Poverty and isolation**: Countries that experience civil war often get locked into high levels of military spending and infectious disease, brain and money drain, low growth and entrenched poverty.

Conflicts can also be felt outside the countries directly involved. Neighbouring States and even the rest of the world suffer immediate and long-term consequences:

- **Refugees**: Providing assistance to refugees can strain the economies and health-care systems of neighbouring countries, which often are poor themselves.

See World Bank, available from http://youthink.worldbank.org/

Conflict destroys homes, tools and fields, exposing survivors to a myriad of threats and depriving them of their means of survival. ■ UN PHOTO/MILTON GRANT

■ **Infectious diseases**: Refugees often spread diseases like malaria, HIV and tuberculosis.

■ **Economic costs**: Neighbouring countries see their investments dry up and their economic growth decline, making it possible for an existing civil war to spark others or evolve into a regional conflict.

■ **Drugs**: About 95 per cent of drug production occurs in countries experiencing civil war, because it is easier to produce large quantities of drugs in places outside the control of a recognized government.

■ **HIV/AIDS**: Combatants use mass rape as a weapon to scare and harm civilians, who in turn can contract HIV or other diseases and unknowingly spread infections.

■ **International terrorism**: Territories without recognized and functional governments become havens for terrorist groups to set up headquarters and training grounds.

THE UNITED NATIONS: CREATED TO KEEP PEACE

The United Nations serves as a global forum where countries can raise and discuss the most difficult issues, including problems of war and peace. When government leaders talk to each other face-to-face, they establish a dialogue, which can result in agreement on how to settle a dispute peacefully. When many countries speak with one voice, by consensus, it creates a global pressure on all. The Secretary-General may also advance a dialogue between and among nations, either directly or through a representative.

Preventing conflict

The United Nations has helped prevent many conflicts from flaring up into full-scale wars. It has also negotiated the peaceful settlement of conflicts and on many occasions helped defuse hostilities, for example during the Berlin crisis (1948-1949), the Cuban missile crisis (1962) and the 1973 Middle East crisis. In each of these cases, United Nations intervention helped prevent war between super powers.

The United Nations also played a major role in ending wars in the Congo (1964), between Iran and Iraq (1988), and in El Salvador (1992) and Guatemala (1996). United Nations-led peace settlements have brought sustained economic growth in Mozambique (1994) and independence to Timor-Leste (2002), and in December 2005, the Organization successfully completed its peacekeeping mandate in Sierra Leone.

Other accomplishments

The United Nations Transition Assistance Group (UNTAG) supervised Namibia's first free and fair elections, which led to its independence between 1989 and 1990.

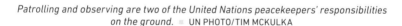

Patrolling and observing are two of the United Nations peacekeepers' responsibilities on the ground. ■ UN PHOTO/TIM MCKULKA

The United Nations Transitional Authority in Cambodia (UNTAC) monitored the ceasefire and the withdrawal of foreign forces from that country, worked with the Cambodian State to set up democratic institutions and organized a free and fair election between 1992 and 1993.

In the former Yugoslavia, the United Nations Protection Force (UNPROFOR) worked to safeguard civilians in demilitarized zones and enable the delivery of humanitarian assistance during the conflict in the 1990s. Initially established in Croatia, the UNPROFOR mandate was later extended to Bosnia and Herzegovina to support delivery of humanitarian relief, and then to the Former Yugoslav Republic of Macedonia for preventive monitoring of borders.

What happens when a country ignores the decisions of the Security Council?

When a country does not comply with the decisions of the Security Council, the Council may take several actions to ensure their implementation. If a country threatens or breaches the peace or commits an act of aggression, the Council may impose economic and trade sanctions, arms and travel bans or diplomatic restrictions. It can also authorize the use of force in certain instances, but that is typically a last resort, to be used only if all peaceful means of settling a dispute have been exhausted.

The Security Council can authorize a coalition of Member States to use "all necessary means," including military action, to deal with a conflict. Examples of this include:

- In 1991, to restore the sovereignty of Kuwait after its invasion by Iraq.
- In 1992, to secure the environment for humanitarian relief to be delivered in Somalia.
- In 1994, to restore the democratically elected government in Haiti.
- In 1999, to restore peace and security in East Timor (Timor-Leste).

PEACEKEEPING AND PEACEBUILDING

Peacekeeping has traditionally been defined as the use of multinational military forces, under United Nations command, to help control and resolve conflicts between countries. Peacekeeping operations fulfil the role of a neutral third party: they help create and maintain ceasefires and form a buffer zone between warring groups. They also provide a wide range of services, such as electoral assistance, training for local police forces, humanitarian action and help in clearing deadly landmines.

While peacekeepers maintain order on the ground, mediators from the United Nations meet with leaders from the disputing parties and try to reach a peaceful solution.

FOCUS ON

The United Nations and the Libya civil war

On 17 March 2011, the Security Council approved a "no-fly zone" over Libya, authorizing "all necessary measures" to protect civilians from being attacked by forces loyal to the Gaddafi regime, which was eventually deposed in October of the same year. A number of United Nations Member States joined in the military efforts needed to implement the Council's resolution.

In September 2011, just as the civil war was about to end, the Council agreed to deploy a mission to Libya to support the country's transitional authorities in their reconstruction efforts, which include restoring human rights and the rule of law, drafting a new constitution, promoting reconciliation and preparing for democratic elections. The United Nations Support Mission in Libya (UNSMIL) is not a military mission but a political one, led by the United Nations Department of Political Affairs. In 2017, for example, the United Nations helped rehabilitate the hospital in Benghazi and trained women in post-war reconstruction.

There are two types of peacekeeping operations: observer missions and peacekeeping forces. Observers are not armed, while soldiers of United Nations peacekeeping forces carry light weapons, which they may use only in self-defence.

Peacekeepers are easily identifiable by the United Nations insignia and the blue berets they wear when on duty. The blue helmet, which has become the symbol of United Nations peacekeepers, is carried during all operations and worn when there is danger. Peacekeepers wear their own national uniforms.

MORE INFO

Peacebuilding

Peacebuilding usually succeeds peacekeeping and refers to efforts to assist countries and regions in their transitions from war to peace, including activities and programmes to support and strengthen these transitions. A peacebuilding process normally begins with the signing of a peace agreement by former warring parties and a United Nations role in facilitating its success. The United Nations, through its presence in a country in transition, ensures that difficulties are overcome through negotiation rather than a resort to arms. At the heart of peacebuilding is the attempt to build a new and legitimate State that will have the capacity to peacefully manage disputes, protect its civilians and ensure respect for human rights. Peacebuilding has played a major role in United Nations operations in Bosnia and Herzegovina, Burundi, Cambodia, El Salvador, Guatemala, Kosovo, Sierra Leone and Timor-Leste, just to cite a few examples.

Governments that volunteer personnel retain ultimate control over their own military forces serving under the United Nations flag.

Commanding the peacekeeping operations

Peacekeeping operations are established by the Security Council and directed by the Secretary-General, often through a special representative. When a conflict is first brought before the Council, it usually asks the parties to reach an agreement by peaceful means. If fighting breaks out or persists, the Council tries to secure a ceasefire. Once the ceasefire is secured, it may then send a peacekeeping mission to the troubled area.

Does the United Nations have an army?

No, the United Nations has no standing international police or military force. Troops who serve in the United Nations peacekeeping operations are voluntarily contributed by the Member States. Civilians, often drawn from among the United Nations staff, also play a key role in forming such operations.

There when the world needs them

United Nations peacekeepers make a difference where it matters most. Peacekeeping operations are initiated in response to serious military or humanitarian crises.

Zambian peacekeepers from the United Nations Mission in Sudan (UNMIS). ■ UN PHOTO/STUART PRICE

Blue helmets are part of the peacekeepers' equipment and also the nickname for peacekeeping personnel. ◼ UN PHOTO/MARCO DORMINO

The environments into which recent peacekeeping operations have been deployed are among the most difficult and least predictable in the world. These are often extremely hostile and volatile areas where violence is likely to flare up at any given moment, for any reason. United Nations peacekeeping missions deploy where others cannot or are not willing to go and so play a vital role in providing a bridge to stability and eventual peace and development.

In the past, peacekeepers were mainly involved in keeping peace between warring nations. Today, conflict has increasingly become an internal affair as many nations are at war with themselves. Due to civil strife and ethnic conflicts, some governments are unable to exercise authority over large portions of their own territory, causing great human suffering. In such situations, the

DID YOU KNOW

United Nations peacekeeping in numbers

- 70 years of peacekeeping (1948-2018).
- 16 current peacekeeping operations (as of 31 December 2017).
- Over 112,294 people, including close to 95,544 uniformed personnel from 127 countries (as of 30 June 2017), over 15,100 civilian personnel, and about 1,600 United Nations Volunteers.
- 3,599 fatalities (as of 30 June 2017).
- A Nobel Peace Prize (1988).
- $7.87 billion: total approved budget for 1 July 2016-30 June 2017.
- Women make up 30 per cent of civilian, 10 per cent of police and 3 per cent of military peacekeepers today.

United Nations is often asked to do two jobs: on the one hand, negotiate a settlement, and on the other, provide emergency relief to the people affected by the conflict. Working under difficult conditions, the United Nations integrates humanitarian assistance with efforts to resolve the crisis, so that people can once again live their lives free from fear.

A cost-effective solution

United Nations peacekeeping operations are far less expensive than other forms of international intervention, and their costs are shared more equitably among Member States. The approved peacekeeping budget for the period from 1 July 2016 to 30 June 2017 was approximately $7.87 billion. This represents less than 0.5 per cent of global military spending (estimated at $1.68 trillion in 2017).

When United Nations costs per peacekeeper are compared to the costs of troops deployed by the United States, other developed States, or regional organizations, the United Nations is the least expensive option by far.

Top 10 contributors of uniformed personnel to United Nations Peacekeeping Operations (June 2017)

1. Ethiopia	8.5%
2. India	7.9%
3. Pakistan	7.4%
4. Bangladesh	7.2%
5. Rwanda	6.4%
6. Nepal	5.4%
7. Egypt	3.2%
8. Burkina Faso	3.0%
9. Senegal	2.9%
10. Ghana	2.8%
Other Member States	45.0%

Financing the United Nations peacekeeping missions

The United Nations peacekeeping budget is funded by Member States.

The first United Nations peacekeeping operation

In November 1947, the United Nations General Assembly endorsed a plan for the partition of Palestine, providing for the creation of an Arab State and a Jewish State, with Jerusalem to be placed under international control. Palestinian Arabs and Arab States refused to accept the plan. On 14 May 1948, the United Kingdom relinquished its mandate over Palestine, and the State of Israel was proclaimed. The next day, the Palestinian Arabs and Arab States began fighting against Israel.

Shortly thereafter, the Security Council called for a cessation of hostilities in Palestine and decided that the truce should be supervised by the United

UNTSO officers supervise armistice between Israel and Arab States in 1959. ▪ UN PHOTO/JG

Nations Mediator, with the assistance of a group of military observers. The first group of military observers, which has become known as the United Nations Truce Supervision Organization (UNTSO), arrived in the region in June 1948. In August 1949, the Security Council assigned new functions to UNTSO in line with the armistice agreements between Israel and its four neighbouring Arab countries—Egypt, Jordan, Lebanon and the Syrian Arab Republic. UNTSO's activities thus were spread throughout five States in the region.

UNTSO is the first-ever United Nations peacekeeping operation, and also the one with the longest history: to this day, its military observers remain in the region to monitor ceasefires and supervise agreements.

Three examples of peacekeeping operations

In the first 40 years of its history (1945-1985), the United Nations established 13 peacekeeping operations. Since then, peacekeeping missions have multiplied.

United Nations Mission in the Republic of South Sudan (UNMISS)

The Security Council voted unanimously to establish a new mission in South Sudan on 8 July 2011, the eve of the country's independence. UNMISS has an authorized budget for up to 7,000 military personnel and 900 police personnel, as well as a civilian component. The new mission took over from the old United Nations Mission in Sudan (UNMIS), which was created following the signing of the 2005 Comprehensive Peace Agreement (CPA) that ended the Sudanese north-south civil war and paved the way for the independence of South Sudan.

The mandate of UNMISS is to consolidate peace and security and help establish conditions for development. The mission aims to strengthen the capacity of the Government of the Republic of South Sudan to rule effectively and democratically and establish good relations with its neighbours.

United Nations-African Union Mission in Darfur (UNAMID)

The Security Council authorized a joint African Union/United Nations hybrid operation in Darfur (UNAMID) on 31 July 2007. The Council commissioned UNAMID to take necessary action to support the implementation of the Darfur Peace Agreement, as well as to protect the country's civilian populations. The Council decided that UNAMID would start implementing its mandated tasks no later than 31 December 2007.

United Nations Stabilization Mission in Haiti (MINUSTAH)

The United Nations Stabilization Mission in Haiti (MINUSTAH) was established on 1 June 2004. It succeeded a Multinational Interim Force (MIF) authorized by the Security Council in February 2004, after an armed conflict that spread to several cities across the country caused President Jean-Bertrand Aristide to leave Haiti for exile. MINUSTAH's mandate is to restore a secure and stable environment, promote democracy and the rule of law, strengthen Haiti's governmental institutions and promote and protect human rights.

The devastating earthquake of 12 January 2010, which resulted in more than 220,000 deaths, including those of 102 United Nations personnel, delivered a severe blow to the country's already shaky economy and infrastructure. Since then, MINUSTAH has continued to fulfil its mandate in difficult circumstances.

CREATING A SUSTAINABLE ENVIRONMENT FOR PEACE

The United Nations work for peace is not limited to the successful conclusion of a peacekeeping mission.

Do we need the United Nations to work for peace?

The world has witnessed more than 50 wars in the past 65 years. Some 17 major armed conflicts were waged around the world in 2017 alone. Luckily, none of them turned into a devastating world war. There is general agreement that the United Nations campaigning for peace and disarmament played a key role in this regard.

There is consensus that the United Nations should be made stronger so that it can stop smaller wars and carry out its decisions fully. But the effectiveness of United Nations actions depends on the political will of the Member States— on their readiness to respect and enforce the decisions they themselves take. Also, these operations require funding from States. Because of a lack of funds, the United Nations is often unable to play a greater role.

The strength of the United Nations comes from its refusal to give up, even in the face of the most difficult challenge. When countries at war do not have the political will to stop fighting, the United Nations must sometimes withdraw its peacekeeping troops. It continues its work, however, through diplomacy and negotiations, constantly speaking with the parties concerned. When conditions are better, the peacekeepers may return.

The world has a long way to go before it can ensure total peace and justice for everyone. Wars, poverty and human rights violations are still widespread. But that is precisely why we need the United Nations. Some say that if the United Nations didn't exist, the countries of the world would have to create another organization, maybe with another name, to do exactly what the United Nations does.

Peacemaking, peacebuilding, peacekeeping, and nation building

In the aftermath of a conflict, the United Nations helps displaced persons and refugees return to their homes. It clears mines, repairs roads and bridges and provides economic and technical help to rebuild the economy. It also monitors elections and closely follows how a country respects the human rights of its citizens. This process, also known as peacebuilding, has helped over 60 countries build democratic institutions. Peacebuilding provides all that is needed to support a country as it moves from war to peace and a functioning self-government.

FOCUS ON

The Peacebuilding Commission

The United Nations has played a vital role in reducing the level of conflict in several regions by mediating peace agreements and assisting in their implementation. Roughly half of all countries that emerge from war lapse back into violence within a few years, driving home the message that, to prevent conflict, peace agreements must be implemented in a sustained manner over time.

The United Nations Peacebuilding Commission helps countries transition from war to lasting peace. The Commission forms the connecting link between peacekeeping and post-conflict operations. Its job is to bring together all the major actors in a situation to discuss and decide on a long-term peacebuilding strategy. What that means is that assistance is better coordinated, money is better spent and there is real coordination between immediate post-conflict efforts and long-term recovery and development.

Peacekeeping, as previously discussed, is organized around a military deployment. It is often a central part of the peacebuilding effort.

Nation-building means different things to different people and is not a term used by the United Nations. It normally refers to a longer historical process that includes the creation of a national identity.

Peacemaking refers to the use of diplomacy to persuade parties in conflict to cease hostilities and negotiate a peaceful settlement of their dispute. All the types of action that can be used for preventive purposes, such as diplomatic peacekeeping, humanitarian aid and peacebuilding, have a role in creating conditions for successful peacemaking.

Children and armed conflicts

Children are unfortunately primary victims of armed conflicts. They are both its targets and increasingly its instruments.

Their suffering takes many forms during and after conflict. They are killed or maimed, orphaned, abducted, deprived of food, education and health care, often drugged, and left with deep emotional scars and trauma.

Boys and girls, some as young as seven years old, are recruited and used as child soldiers, forced to enact the hatred of adults. Girls face additional risks, particularly sexual violence and exploitation.

Around 300,000 children, boys and girls between the ages of 7 and 18 are involved in conflicts around the world. ■ UN PHOTO/SILVAIN LIECHTI

Child soldiers

It has been estimated that around 300,000 boys and girls under the age of 18 have been involved in conflicts around the world in the past two decades alone. Children are used as combatants, cooks, porters, messengers, spies, human mine detectors, sexual slaves, forced labourers and even suicide bombers. Physically vulnerable and easily intimidated, children typically make obedient soldiers. Many are abducted or recruited by force and often compelled to follow orders under threat of death. Others join armed groups out of desperation. As society breaks down during conflict, children lose access to school and are driven from their homes or separated from their families. Many perceive armed groups as their best chance for survival. Others seek to escape from poverty or join military forces to avenge family members who have been killed.

Collaborative efforts between the Office of the Special Representative of the Secretary-General for Children and Armed Conflict, UNICEF and other key United Nations entities, as well as Member States, regional organizations, non-government organizations (NGOs) and civil society groups, have resulted in significant advances and tangible results for children.

FOCUS ON

Sport for development and peace

Sport has historically played an important role in all societies, be it in the form of competitive sport, physical activity or play. But what does sport have to do with the United Nations?

The **United Nations Office on Sport for Development and Peace (UNOSDP)** provides the entry point to the United Nations system on Sport for Development and Peace, bringing the worlds of sport and development closer together.

Sport has a unique power to attract, mobilize and inspire. By its very nature, sport is about participation, about inclusion and citizenship. It stands for human values such as respect for the opponent, acceptance of binding rules, teamwork and fairness, all of which are principles also contained in the Charter of the United Nations. It is therefore not surprising that many United Nations Goodwill Ambassadors are internationally renowned sports players.

Because of its properties of integration and post-trauma relief, and because it brings life back to normal even for a short while, the United Nations also uses sport to reach out to those most in need—refugees, child soldiers, victims of conflict and natural catastrophes, the impoverished, persons with disabilities, victims of racism, stigmatization and discrimination, persons living with HIV/AIDS and other diseases.

Sporting tournament in South Sudan. ■ UN PHOTO/JC MCILWAINE

Returning children to civilian life and hopefully to their families

UNICEF works to release children from armed forces and groups as soon as possible, even during conflict, and help them return to their families. As part of this, UNICEF supports services that care for the physical and mental health and well-being of such children, providing them with life skills and engaging them in positive activities oriented towards their future. These programmes adopt a community-based approach that includes support for other vulnerable children who have also been affected by conflict to promote reconciliation and avoid discrimination. These actions require a long-term perspective and a long-term commitment to both the children and the conflict-affected communities to which they return.

In 2015, as many as 15 million children were caught up in violent conflicts in the Central African Republic, Iraq, South Sudan, the State of Palestine, Syria and Ukraine—including those internally displaced or living as refugees. Globally, an estimated 230 million children currently live in countries and areas affected by armed conflicts.

A GLOBAL COUNTER-TERRORISM STRATEGY

The United Nations has long been active in the fight against international terrorism. Reflecting the determination of the world to eliminate this threat, the Organization and its agencies have developed a wide range of legal instruments that enable the international community to take action to suppress terrorism and bring those responsible for acts of terror to justice.

Some 19 international legal instruments have been negotiated through the United Nations between 1963 and 2017, including treaties against hostage-taking, airplane hijacking, terrorist bombings and financing terrorism. A Security Council Counter-Terrorism Committee oversees how Member States carry out the commitments they made after the attacks of 11 September 2001, and works to increase their capability to fight terrorism.

The United Nations General Assembly adopted a Global Counter-Terrorism Strategy on 8 September 2006. The Strategy—in the form of a resolution and an annexed plan of action—is a unique instrument that enhances national, regional and international efforts to counter terrorism. Its adoption marks the first time that all Member States have agreed on a common strategic and operational approach to fighting terrorism. Important initiatives include:

- Improving the efficiency of counter-terrorism technical cooperation between countries so that all States can play their parts effectively.

- Putting in place systems to assist victims of terrorism and their families.

- Addressing the threat of bioterrorism by establishing a single comprehensive database on biological incidents, focusing on improving States' public health systems and acknowledging the need to bring together major stakeholders to ensure that biotechnological advances are not used for terrorist or other criminal purposes but for public good.

- Involving civil society, regional and subregional organizations in the fight against terrorism and developing partnerships with the private sector to prevent terrorist attacks on particularly vulnerable targets.

- Exploring innovative means to address the growing threat of terrorists' use of the Internet.

Terror attack destroys part of United Nations Headquarters in Bagdad in 2003. ■ UN PHOTO/AP

- Modernizing border and customs control systems and improving the security of travel documents to prevent terrorists from travelling and stop the movement of dangerous and illicit materials.

- Enhancing cooperation to combat money-laundering and the financing of terrorism.

United Nations Member States agreed to strengthen the role of the United Nations System in combatting terrorism while maintaining respect for human rights for all and the rule of law as the fundamental basis in that struggle.

DISARMAMENT

Disarmament is often linked to weapons of mass destruction such as nuclear warheads and chemical and biological weapons, but it goes further than that. In today's world, most of the arms used are small and light, and can be wielded by an individual or a group of two or three people. Disarmament also comprises efforts to reduce the number of these smaller, and therefore more easily transportable, weapons.

The impact of armed violence

Armed violence—the intentional, threatened or actual use of weapons to inflict injury or death—takes many forms, from political to criminal to interpersonal, and appears in a wide range of contexts. Armed violence does not just happen in areas of conflict. It is widespread, and every region of the world is affected. It imposes a tremendous emotional and economic burden on individuals, families and communities worldwide.

Across all affected societies, young males, at the peak of their productive lives, are the most common perpetrators, as well as immediate victims, of armed attacks. Women and pre-adolescent boys and girls also suffer as both direct and indirect victims of armed violence.

It is estimated that roughly 750,000 people have died in recent years as a result of the violence associated with armed conflicts and large- and small-scale criminality. Two thirds of these deaths occur outside war zones. In addition, as many as seven million people are injured each year, with victims often suffering permanent disabilities and living with profound psychological as well as physical scars.

Armed violence not only destroys lives; it also has a negative effect on the economy, damaging infrastructure and property, limiting the delivery of public services, undermining investment in human, social and economic capital and contributing to unproductive expenditures on security services. Because of trafficking and major population displacements, it is both a domestic and international security concern. Moreover, it undermines development and constitutes an impediment to the achievement of the United Nations Sustainable Development Goals.

The "Knotted Gun," a symbol of peace, is the creation of artist Karl Fredrik Reutersward, offered to the United Nations by the Government of Luxembourg. ▪ UN PHOTO

Controlling small arms and light weapons

Most violent conflicts today are fought within States, primarily with small arms and light weapons. Up to 8 million small arms are produced every year, and their use accounts for 60 to 90 per cent of direct conflict deaths.

Small arms are not in themselves unlawful, and they have legitimate uses, including for national defence and the protection and safety of people and property by law enforcement officials. The value of their global trade, along with their ammunitions, is estimated at more than $7 billion per year. A prohibition is therefore not a solution. The problem lies with undocumented trade, which may run in the billions of dollars, as well as sale at very low cost or the dumping of outdated rms and surplus weapons in the arsenals of other countries. What we need is adequate regulation of their availability and use.

At a United Nations Conference on the Illicit Trade in Small Arms and Light Weapons in 2001, States agreed on measures to strengthen international cooperation in curbing this illegal arms trade. They unanimously adopted the United Nations Programme of Action to Prevent, Combat and Eradicate the Illicit Trade in Small Arms and Light Weapons in All Its Aspects. The Programme contains a wide range of undertakings and actions that Member States have committed themselves to at the national, regional and global levels. These include developing, adopting and strengthening national legislation on small arms and light weapons; destroying weapons that are confiscated, seized or collected; and fostering international cooperation that allows States to identify and trace illicit arms and light weapons.

In 1945, more than 120,000 people were killed in Hiroshima and Nagasaki (Japan) by atomic bombs. The Hiroshima Peace Memorial, the only structure left standing in the area where the first bomb exploded, became a UNESCO World Heritage site in 1996. ■ UN PHOTO/DB

The United Nations and associated entities have collected and documented hundreds of thousands of weapons. These records help improve the understanding of the illicit arms trade and facilitate the monitoring of progress made by post-conflict countries as well as the efficacy of arms-reduction initiatives.

Ensuring world safety by reducing nuclear weapons

Humankind has avoided a nuclear war thanks in large part to the disarmament activities of the United Nations, in particular the push for the elimination of weapons of mass destruction. However, the world remains a dangerous place, as supplies are still growing. More people train for war every day, and the costs of the arms race continue to escalate as brinkmanship in the Korean peninsula and extreme international tensions culminated after the outbreak of hostilities in Crimea and the Donbas in 2014.

After two atomic bombs were dropped on Hiroshima and Nagasaki in Japan, the Second World War (1939-1945) came to an end. Since then, the world has witnessed many wars. These conflicts have killed more than 20 million people, approximately 80 per cent of them civilians. There are now at least eight countries that possess nuclear weapons (nuclear powers). Despite big reductions after the collapse of the Soviet Union, the total stockpile of nuclear weapons in the world in 2017 amounted to approximately 15,200 nuclear warheads, with a combined destructive capability of 150,000 Hiroshima-sized bombs.

Disarmament is an urgent global need

Take a minute to count from 1 to 60, and then consider this: By the time you finish counting, the world has lost 25 to 30 children. During the same time, the world has spent about $3.1 million for military purposes.

Both the accumulation of arms and economic development require large-scale human and material resources. Since resources are limited, pursuing either process tends to happen at the expense of the other. There is growing agreement that, in the long run, the world can either continue the arms race or achieve social and economic development for the benefit of all, but it will not be able to do both.

General and complete disarmament—in other words, the gradual elimination of weapons of mass destruction—is one of the goals set by the United Nations. Its immediate objectives are to eliminate the danger of war, particularly nuclear war, and to implement measures to halt and reverse the arms race.

Some United Nations actions for disarmament

- The Partial Test-Ban Treaty, 1963: prohibits nuclear tests in the atmosphere, in outer space and underwater.

- The Non-Proliferation Treaty, 1968: prohibits the spread of nuclear weapons from nuclear to non-nuclear countries.

- The Chemical Weapons Convention, 1992: prohibits the use, manufacturing and stockpiling of such weapons.

- The Comprehensive Nuclear-Test-Ban Treaty, 1996: bans all underground nuclear test explosions.

- The Anti-Personnel Landmines Convention, 1997: prohibits the use, stockpiling, production and transfer of such mines.

- The Convention on Cluster Munitions, 2008: prohibits the use, stockpiling, production and transfer of such weapons.

- The new, bilateral Strategic Arms Reduction Treaty (New START), 2010: requires the United States and the Russian Federation to reduce their deployed strategic warheads to no more than 1,550 each.

- **The landmark Arms Trade Treaty (ATT)**: regulating the international trade in conventional arms—from small arms to battle tanks, combat aircraft and warships—entered into force on 24 December 2014.

Battling cluster munitions and landmines

Since the 1980s, the United Nations has been addressing the problems posed by millions of deadly landmines scattered in over 60 countries. Each year thousands of people—most of them children, women and the elderly—are maimed

This 13-year old girl lost both legs to a mine. ■ UN PHOTO/UNHCR/ROGER LEMOYNE

or killed by these "silent killers." Meanwhile, new landmines continue to be deployed in various countries around the world.

The United Nations Mine Action Service (UNMAS) acts as the focal point for mine action and coordinates all mine-related activities of United Nations agencies, funds and programmes. The work focuses on mine clearance, mine awareness, risk-reduction education, victim assistance and stockpile destruction.

Since the anti-personnel mine ban treaty went into force in 1999, the number of new victims each year has dropped, large tracts of land have been cleared, and the number of stockpiled mines has decreased by millions. The treaty has had a major impact on the global landmine problem. It has not, however, addressed another large problem: explosive remnants of war (ERW), which kill thousands of civilians annually. "Explosive remnants of war" refers to aban-

FOCUS ON

Mine terror and action in numbers

- Number of countries affected by landmines and explosive remnants of war in 2015: 64 States or territories.

- Number of people estimated to have been killed or maimed by landmines in the last 30 years: over one million, of which 71 per cent were civilians and 32 per cent children.

- Number of new casualties in 2015: 6,461 people have been wounded or killed by land mines and other explosive remnants of war primarily in Afghanistan, Iraq, Libya, Syria, Ukraine and Yemen.

doned bombs and grenades but also cluster munitions, which fail to detonate but remain volatile and dangerous. United Nations-supported mine-action programmes help countries eliminate the threat of landmines and explosive remnants of war. An international movement seeking to limit the use of cluster munitions (weapons that contain and release many smaller explosive devices at the same time) has gained momentum in recent years.

THE NOBEL PEACE PRIZE AND THE UNITED NATIONS

The Norwegian Nobel Committee awarded the 2001 Nobel Peace Prize in equal portions to the United Nations and its Secretary-General, Kofi Annan, "for their work for a better-organized and more peaceful world."

In addition, the Nobel Committee honoured the United Nations System with the Peace Prize as follows:

2007 | The United Nations Intergovernmental Panel on Climate Change (IPCC) and Al Gore, former Vice-President of the United States

2005 | The International Atomic Energy Agency (IAEA) and Mohamed ElBaradei, IAEA Director General

2001 | The United Nations and Kofi Annan, United Nations Secretary-General

1988 | The United Nations Peacekeeping Forces

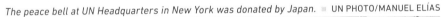

The peace bell at UN Headquarters in New York was donated by Japan. ■ UN PHOTO/MANUEL ELÍAS

1981 | The Office of the United Nations High Commissioner for Refugees (UNHCR) (second time)

1974 | Seán MacBride, United Nations Commissioner for Namibia

1969 | The International Labour Organization (ILO)

1965 | The United Nations Children's Fund (UNICEF)

1961 | Dag Hammarskjöld, United Nations Secretary-General

1957 | Lester Bowles Pearson, Canadian statesman, for striving to end the Suez Crisis and Middle East question through the United Nations

1954 | The Office of the United Nations High Commissioner for Refugees (UNHCR)

1951 | Léon Jouhaux, a founder of the International Labour Organization

1950 | Ralph Bunche, United Nations Trusteeship Director

1949 | Lord John Boyd Orr, founding Director-General of the United Nations Food and Agricultural Organization (FAO)

1945 | Cordell Hull, United States Secretary of State and instrumental in establishing the United Nations

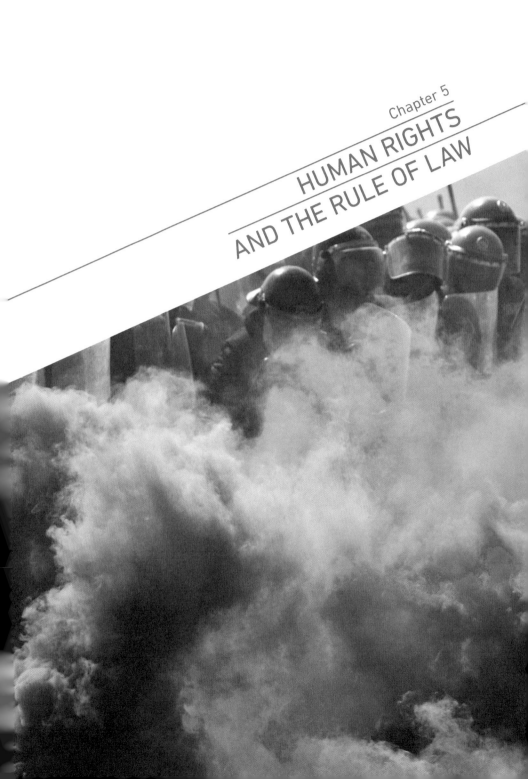

Chapter 5
HUMAN RIGHTS
AND THE RULE OF LAW

QUICK FACTS ABOUT HUMAN RIGHTS

- The Charter of the United Nations, which came into force on 24 October 1945, and the **Universal Declaration of Human Rights**, which was adopted in 1948, proclaim the equal rights of all men and women and of all nations, large and small.

- One of the great achievements of the United Nations is the creation of a large body of **human rights law**—a universal and internationally protected code to which all nations must subscribe and all people aspire.

- The **Convention on the Rights of the Child**, which entered into force in 1989, exists to protect and promote the rights of girls and boys everywhere in the world.

- The United Nations has defined a broad range of internationally accepted rights, including **civil, cultural, economic, political and social**. It has also established mechanisms to promote and protect these rights and to assist States in carrying out these responsibilities.

- United Nations legal instruments have banned the participation of **children under 18 in armed conflict** and prohibited the trafficking of children.

- Although two-thirds of countries have abolished the **death penalty**, at least 1,032 executions occurred in 2016. That is a drop from the 26-year high of 1,634 documented in 2015.

- In 2014, about 61 million school-aged children were **out of school**, an overwhelming proportion of them in sub-Saharan Africa and Southern Asia. Of the world's estimated 758 million illiterate adults, two-thirds are women who are denied the right to an education.

- Several governments monitor their citizens' Internet use and have censored or imprisoned them for freely **expressing opinions** online.

- Roughly 168 million children remain trapped in **child labour**. Over half of them are exposed to hazardous environments, slavery, prostitution, drug trafficking, armed conflict and other illicit activities.

HUMAN RIGHTS: WHAT ARE THEY?

ALL human beings are born **free** and **equal** in dignity and rights.

Article 1, Universal Declaration of Human Rights

Definition

Human rights are those rights that are essential for us to live as human beings. They are rights inherent to all people, regardless of race, colour, gender, language, religion, political or other opinion, national or social origin, property, birth or other status. Without human rights, we cannot fully develop and use our human qualities, our intelligence, talent and creativity.

All human rights—whether they are civil and political rights, such as the right to life, equality before the law and freedom of expression; economic, social and cultural rights, such as the rights to work, social security and education; or collective rights, such as the rights to development and self-determination—are indivisible, interrelated and interdependent. Without human rights, countries cannot fully develop their potential and therefore better standards of life will not be reached.

Cambodia Genocide museum documents Khmer Rouge brutality. ■ UN PHOTO/MARK GARTEN

What are our human rights?

All people have the right to:

- Life, liberty and security
- Freedom of expression
- Freedom from slavery
- Fair trial
- Equal treatment before the law
- Equal protection under the law
- Freedom from arbitrary arrest, detention and exile
- Freedom of movement
- Protection of private life
- A nationality
- Freely contract a marriage and start a family

- Freedom of thought, conscience and religion
- Freedom of opinion
- Freedom of association
- Social security
- Work
- Equal pay for equal work
- Rest and leisure
- A standard of living sufficient to guarantee health and well-being
- Education
- Take part in the cultural life of the community
- Protection of their intellectual property

Characteristics of human rights

Human rights are:

- **Universal**: They should be respected for all individuals across all boundaries and civilizations.

- **Inalienable**: They should not be taken away, except in specific situations and according to due process, as in the case of a person found guilty of a crime after a fair trial.

- **Interdependent and indivisible**: The improvement of one right facilitates advancement of the others. Likewise, the deprivation of one right adversely affects the others.

- **Equal and non-discriminatory**: The rights of all people should be respected, regardless of their race, colour, gender, language, religion, opinion, origin or status.

- **Both rights and obligations**: States assume the obligation under international law to respect, protect and fulfil human rights. At the individual level, we are entitled to our own human rights, and we must also respect the human rights of others.

THE UNITED NATIONS AND HUMAN RIGHTS

The Universal Declaration of Human Rights

The idea of human rights did not begin with the establishment of the United Nations; its roots can be found across world cultures and religions. However, the adoption of the Universal Declaration of Human Rights by the United Nations General Assembly on 10 December 1948 was a landmark achievement in world history, as it was the first time that the international community set down formal standards of human rights and freedoms that should be enjoyed by everyone, everywhere.

The General Assembly called upon all Member States to publicize the text of the Declaration and "to cause it to be disseminated, displayed, read and expounded principally in schools and other educational institutions, without distinction based on the political status of countries or territories".

By this Declaration, governments accepted the obligation to ensure that all human beings—womsen and men, rich and poor, strong and weak, young and old, of all races and religions—are treated equally. The Declaration is not part of binding international law, but due to universal acceptance by countries around the world, it has gained immense moral weight and inspired both human rights development and a rich body of legally binding international human rights treaties.

Human rights law

The United Nations has been the driving force behind more than 80 human rights treaties and declarations for the rights of women, children, disabled persons, minorities, indigenous people and other more vulnerable groups. Together, these agreements have helped create a culture of human rights

DID YOU KNOW

The most translated document in the world

The Office of the High Commissioner for Human Rights has been awarded the Guinness World Record for having collected, translated and disseminated the Universal Declaration of Human Rights into more than 380 languages and dialects, from Abkhaz to Zulu. The Universal Declaration is thus the document most translated—indeed, the most universal—in the world. All translations are available from www.ohchr.org.

The United Nations has adopted a multitude of international human rights treaties and conventions, the most important of which are the two International Covenants—one on economic, social and cultural rights and the other on civil and political rights. The Universal Declaration, together with the two Covenants and their Optional Protocols, constitute the International Bill of Human Rights.

Eleanor Roosevelt, former first lady of the United States, was one of the authors of the Universal Declaration of Human Rights in 1948. ■ UN PHOTO

throughout the world, which has proved to be a powerful tool in curbing abuses and establishing a more just order for humankind, especially for the less powerful among us.

International human rights law lays down obligations that States are bound to respect. By becoming parties to international treaties, States agree to refrain from interfering with the enjoyment of human rights and to protect individuals and groups against abuses. By ratifying treaties, governments commit to adopting national measures and legislation compatible with the terms laid out in the treaties. A country's domestic legal system therefore provides the principal legal protection of human rights guaranteed under international law.

When domestic legal proceedings fail to address human rights abuses, mechanisms for individual and group complaints are available at the regional and international levels. Under a confidential communications procedure, allegations of gross and systematic violations of human rights can also be submitted to the United Nations if domestic remedies have been exhausted and there is no possibility for obtaining justice in one's own country.

Other International Human Rights Instruments[1]

- Convention on Consent to Marriage, Minimum Age for Marriage and Registration of Marriages (1962).

- International Convention on the Elimination of All Forms of Racial Discrimination (1965).

---

[1]   A complete list of international instruments can be found at: www.ohchr.org/EN/Issues/IntOrder/Pages/InternationalInstruments.aspx

- Convention on the Elimination of All Forms of Discrimination against Women (1979).

- Convention against Torture and Other Cruel, Inhuman or Degrading Treatment or Punishment (1984).

- Convention on the Rights of the Child (1989).

- International Convention on the Protection of the Rights of All Migrant Workers and Members of their Families (1990).

- United Nations Principles for Older Persons (1991).

- Declaration of Commitment on HIV/AIDS (2001).

- International Convention for the Protection of All Persons from Enforced Disappearance (2006).

- Convention on the Rights of Persons with Disabilities (2006).

The legal status of these instruments varies. On the one hand, declarations, principles, guidelines, standard rules and recommendations have no binding legal effect, although they do have an undeniable moral force and provide practical guidance for governments. On the other hand, covenants, statutes, protocols and conventions are legally binding for those States that ratify or accede to them.

Who is responsible for human rights at the United Nations?

Every United Nations body and agency is involved to some degree in the protection of human rights. However, the main United Nations group responsible for promoting and protecting human rights is the Human Rights Council.

Human Rights Council

The Human Rights Council was created in June 2006 to replace the Human Rights Commission, which had operated since 1946.

RESPONSIBILITIES

The Human Rights Council is the main United Nations forum for dialogue and cooperation on human rights. It is empowered to prevent abuses, inequity and discrimination, protect the most vulnerable people and groups and expose perpetrators all around the world.

HUMAN RIGHTS COUNCIL AND THE GENERAL ASSEMBLY

As a subsidiary body of the General Assembly, the Human Rights Council monitors human rights situations in all countries and is directly accountable to the full membership of the United Nations. It is, however, administered by the United Nations High Commissioner for Human Rights.

The Human Rights Council chamber in Geneva. ■ UN PHOTO/JEAN-MARC FERRÉ

The Human Rights Council is required to make recommendations to the General Assembly for further developing international law in the field of human rights and to undertake a Universal Periodic Review of each State's fulfilment of its human rights obligations and commitments. The Council has the authority to recommend that the General Assembly suspend the rights and privileges of any Member State in the Council that has persistently committed gross and systematic violations of human rights. This process of suspension requires a two-thirds majority vote by the General Assembly.

COMPOSITION AND MEETINGS

The Human Rights Council meets in Geneva for 10 weeks every year. It is composed of 47 elected United Nations Member States, each of which serves for an initial period of three years and cannot be elected for more than two consecutive terms.

High Commissioner for Human Rights

The High Commissioner is the principal United Nations official responsible for human rights. He or she reports directly to the Secretary-General.

The OHCHR leads global human rights efforts and represents the world's commitment to the universal ideals of human rights. It denounces violations worldwide, provides a forum for identifying, highlighting and responding to human rights challenges and acts as the principal focal point of human rights research, education, information and advocacy in the United Nations System.

OHCHR provides assistance—often expertise and technical training in the administration of justice, legislative reform, and the electoral process—to governments, civil society and other United Nations entities and organizations, in order to help them implement international human rights standards on the ground. The Office also assists the Human Rights Council and the committees that monitor the implementation of the core human rights treaties, which may call upon governments to respond to allegations of human rights violations (these committees are referred to as the Treaty Bodies).

Special rapporteurs and working groups

Special rapporteurs and working groups on human rights investigate violations and intervene in individual cases and emergency situations; these are referred to as "special procedures." United Nation human rights experts are independent. They serve in their positions for a maximum of six years and do not get paid for their work. The number of such experts has grown steadily over the years. In 2017, there were 44 thematic and 12 country mandates. Hence, special rapporteurs and working groups are assigned to report either on a specific country or territory or on a theme (for example, the right to food or violence against women).

In preparing their reports for the Human Rights Council and the General Assembly, these experts use all reliable resources, including individual complaints and information from NGOs. They may also initiate "urgent-action procedures" to intercede with governments at the highest level. A significant portion of their research is done in the field, where they meet with authorities and victims and gather on-site evidence of alleged violations and misconduct. Their reports are made public, thus helping to advertise abuses and emphasize the responsibility of governments for the protection of human rights. Apart from a few exceptions, governments do not like to be named and shamed and have rarely refused to let these investigating experts into their countries for fear of a public outcry and tacit recognition of guilt.

International Criminal Court

In 1998, at a conference in Rome, 120 nations established a permanent International Criminal Court (ICC). In creating the Court, the world made it clear that impunity— exemption from punishment—is no longer acceptable. This Court, which came into being in 2002 when its founding treaty (the Rome Statute) came into force, prosecutes individuals for the most serious crimes, such as genocide, war crimes and crimes against humanity. As of September 2017, 124 countries were parties to the International Criminal Court.

The International Criminal Court is independent from the United Nations; however, the Security Council may refer human rights situations to the Court. For example, in 2005, acting on reports of widespread abuses, the Security Council referred the situation in the Darfur region of Sudan to the Court.

A real need exists for such a court. In countries at war, there may be no judicial system capable of dealing with war crimes. Those in power may also be unwilling to prosecute their own citizens for wrongdoing, especially if they are high-ranking. The International Criminal Court provides a just option in such cases, breaking the cycle of impunity.

Other international courts and tribunals

Over the past two decades, the Security Council has established as subsidiary organs two ad hoc, territorially specific, international criminal tribunals to prosecute crimes against humanity in the former Yugoslavia and in Rwanda. There are also three hybrid courts established respectively by Cambodia, Lebanon and Sierra Leone, with substantial help from the United Nations. These are not permanent and would cease to exist once their activities draw to a close.

- The Security Council established the **International Criminal Tribunal for the former Yugoslavia** in 1993, following massive violations of humanitarian law during the fighting in the former Yugoslavia. It was the first war-crimes court created by the United Nations and the first international war-crimes tribunal since the Nuremberg and Tokyo tribunals at the end of the Second World War. The Tribunal tries those individuals most responsible for appalling acts, such as murder, torture, rape, enslavement, destruction of property and other violent crimes. It aims to render justice to thousands of victims and their families, thus contributing to a lasting peace in the area. As of 2017, the Tribunal had indicted 161 people. Since the Tribunal started its work, 78 individuals, or 48 per cent of the 161 accused, had charges of sexual violence included in their indictments.

- The Security Council created the **International Criminal Tribunal for Rwanda** in 1994 to prosecute those responsible for genocide and other serious violations of international humanitarian law committed in Rwanda between 1 January and 31 December 1994. It was also entrusted with the prosecution of Rwandan citizens who had committed acts of genocide and other such violations of international law in the territory of neighbouring States during the same period. In 1998, the Rwanda Tribunal handed down the first-ever verdict by an international court on the crime of genocide, as well as the first-ever sentence for that crime. The Tribunal closed on 31 December 2015. It had indicted 93 individuals for genocide and other serious violations of international humanitarian law.

- The **Special Court for Sierra Leone** was set up jointly by the Government of Sierra Leone and the United Nations. It prosecuted those who bore the greatest responsibility for serious violations of international humanitarian and Sierra Leonean law since 30 November 1996. The Residual Special Court for Sierra Leone was further established to oversee the continuing legal obligations of the Special Court for Sierra Leone after its closure in 2013.

■ The Extraordinary Chambers in the Courts of Cambodia for the Prosecution of Crimes Committed during the Period of Democratic Kampuchea were created jointly by the Government of Cambodia and the United Nations, but are independent of both of them. The Cambodian court, with international participation, tries significant crimes committed during the Khmer Rouge regime (1975-1979), which killed up to 3 million people.

■ The **Special** Tribunal **for Lebanon** prosecutes those who bear responsibility for the terrorist attack of 14 February 2005, in the Lebanese capital Beirut, which resulted in the death of Lebanese Prime Minister Rafiq Hariri and the death or injury of many others.

THE RIGHT TO DEVELOPMENT FOR ALL

Development as a right

The right to development is at the very heart of the United Nations's efforts to promote and protect human rights. It is the focus of the 1986 Declaration on the Right to Development and is also highlighted in several other documents, including the 1992 Rio Declaration on Environment and Development, the 2000 Millennium Declaration and the 2030 Agenda with its Sustainable Development Goals, which emphasize a symbiotic relationship with the right to development.

Declaration on the Right to Development

Development is a human right. Widening poverty gaps, food shortages, climate change, economic crises, armed conflicts, rising unemployment, popular uprisings, corruption of elites and other pressing challenges confront our world today. To respond effectively, the United Nations adopted the Declaration on the Right to Development, which unequivocally establishes development as a right and puts people at the centre of the development process.

The Declaration states that everyone is "entitled to participate in, contribute to, and enjoy economic, social, cultural and political development, in which all human rights and fundamental freedoms can be fully realized". Yet today, 25 years later, many children, women and men still live in dire need. Their entitlement to a life of dignity, freedom and equal opportunity remains unfulfilled. This directly affects the realization of a wide range of civil, cultural, economic, political and social rights.

The pursuit of economic growth is not an end in itself. The Declaration clearly states that development is an all-encompassing process aiming to improve "the well-being of the entire population and of all individuals on the basis of

Mongolian herders practice sustainable resource management with the help of United Nations Development Programme. ■ UN PHOTO/ESKINDER DEBEBE

their active, free and meaningful participation in development and in the fair distribution" of the resulting benefits.

Like all human rights, the right to development belongs to all individuals and peoples, everywhere, without discrimination and with their participation. The Declaration recognizes the right to self-determination and full sovereignty over natural wealth and resources. The right to development is not about charity; it is about enabling and empowering all women, men and children in their own countries to manage their own resources.

A framework to promote all human rights

Because the right to development comprises all human rights—civil, cultural, economic, political and social, it provides a complete framework for the policies and programmes of all relevant actors in the promotion and protection of human rights at the global, regional, subregional and national levels. The right to development:

- Integrates aspects of both human rights and development theory and practice.

- Involves both national and international dimensions of State responsibilities, including the creation of favourable conditions for development and human rights.

- Demands that human beings be placed at the centre of development policy, that they be active participants and that they be guaranteed social justice and equity.

■ Embodies the human rights principles of equality, non-discrimination, participation, transparency and accountability, as well as international cooperation in an integrated manner.

■ Implies the principles of self-determination and full sovereignty over natural wealth and resources.

■ Facilitates a holistic approach to the issue of poverty by addressing its root causes.

■ Strengthens the advancement of the poorest people with due attention to the rights of the most marginalized.

■ Fosters friendly relations between countries, international solidarity and cooperation and assistance in areas of concern to developing countries.

Rule of law

The concept of rule of law implies a system of governance based on non-arbitrary rules, as opposed to one based on the power and whims of a dictator. It is linked to the principles of justice and equity, involving ideals of accountability and fairness in the protection and vindication of human rights and the prevention and punishment of wrongs.

The United Nations supports the development, promotion and implementation of international norms and standards in most fields of international law. It also promotes the establishment of a rule of law at the national level that includes:

■ A Constitution or its equivalent, as the highest law of the land.

■ A clear and consistent legal system.

■ Strong institutions of justice, governance, security and human rights that are well structured, funded, trained and equipped.

FOCUS ON

The Declaration on the Right to Development in words

"The right to development is an inalienable human right by virtue of which every human person and all peoples are entitled to participate in, contribute to, and enjoy economic, social, cultural and political development, in which all human rights and fundamental freedoms can be fully realized." (Article 1.1)

"The human right to development also implies the full realization of the right of peoples to self-determination, which includes, subject to the relevant provisions of both International Covenants on Human Rights, the exercise of their inalienable right to full sovereignty over all their natural wealth and resources." (Article 1.2)

- Transitional justice processes and mechanisms.

- A public and civil society that is able to hold government officials and institutions accountable.

These are the norms, policies, institutions and processes that form the core of a society in which individuals feel safe and secure. The challenge is to develop a system that is responsive to the needs of ordinary citizens, including the poor, and that promotes development. The electoral and legislative branches must be strong, people must have access to justice and public administration and governments must deliver basic services to all those in need.

Fairness, equity and justice are essential. They promote peace, protect human rights and sustain progress for all.

FOCUS ON

Forced labour and human trafficking

One of the worse violations of human rights today is human trafficking—a crime that strips people of their rights, ruins their dreams and robs them of their dignity. It feeds off poverty and despair, and physically and emotionally harms millions of men, women, boys and girls. Human trafficking is a global problem; no country is immune.

Today (in 2017), almost 21 million people around the world are trapped in forced labour, including debt bondage, human trafficking and other forms of modern slavery. The victims are the most vulnerable people—women and girls forced into prostitution, migrants trapped in debt bondage, sweatshop or farm workers kept there by illegal tactics and paid little or nothing.

A few frightening facts:

- The most common form of human trafficking (79 per cent) is sexual exploitation.

- The victims of sexual exploitation are predominantly women and girls: they account for about 80 per cent of the detected victims.

- In Eastern Europe and Central Asia, women are increasingly trafficking other women; shockingly, former victims become traffickers.

- Worldwide, almost 20 per cent of all trafficking victims are children. However, in some parts of Africa and Southeast Asia, children are the majority (up to 100 per cent in parts of West Africa).

Historically, human trafficking is nothing new. The transatlantic slave trade, which lasted about 400 years, marked one of the darkest chapters in human history. Slavery has existed since antiquity.

Nadia Murad, United Nations Office on Drugs and Crime Goodwill Ambassador for the Dignity of Survivors of Human Trafficking. ■ UN PHOTO/MANUEL ELÍAS

In a country where the rule of law is observed, human rights are respected. The State develops laws to protect its people from those who would violate them, even if the violator is the State itself. The police, lawyers and judges must remain fair and independent. No one can be arrested without serious grounds, detained for long periods awaiting trial or in inhumane conditions.

The judicial and legal process should be transparent, and it most certainly should not include forced disappearances, torture, slavery or executions. Instead, it should offer health services, educational programmes and vocational

FOCUS ON

Helping the victims of torture

Torture by the State is still practiced in many countries. The United Nations wants this to stop.

In 1984, the United Nations adopted the Convention against Torture. A 10-member Committee against Torture periodically examines reports from countries that have ratified the Convention.

Torture is strictly banned but still perpetrated in some countries. Men, women and children continue to be tortured in detention simply for expressing their views, in order to force confessions or just because they were in the wrong place at the wrong time. The United Nations has also set up a Voluntary Fund for Victims of Torture. It provides psychological, medical, social, legal and economic assistance to victims of torture and their children.

trainings for prisoners so that, once freed, they have a chance to get on the right path and care for themselves and their families without committing subsequent offences.

A State governed by the rule of law should keep its people safe from corruption, organized crime, trafficking—in such products as illicit drugs, weapons, rare fauna, flora and ivory products, counterfeit goods, cultural artefacts and human beings—as well as cybercrime, like child pornography and internet bullying, and environmental crime. It also cooperates with others to fight the international war against terrorism. The United Nations offers guidance, support and training to assist States in establishing appropriate policies and institutions and enforcing the rule of law.

Active, Free and Meaningful Participation

The link between democracy and human rights is captured in Article 21 (3) of the Universal Declaration of Human Rights, which states: "The will of the people shall be the basis of the authority of government; this will shall be expressed in periodic and genuine elections which shall be by universal and equal suffrage and shall be held by secret vote or by equivalent free voting procedures."

Democracy is a universal value based on the freely expressed will of people to determine their own political, economic, social and cultural systems and to fully participate in all aspects of their lives. It is as much a process as a goal, and only with the complete support of the international community, national governing bodies, civil society and individuals can the ideal of democracy be made into a reality to be enjoyed by everyone, everywhere.

While democracies share common features, there is no single model. For example, the chief of government can be elected directly by the citizens of the country or indirectly by representatives of the country's constituencies. Sometimes the President is both Head of State and Head of Government, but in other democracies the powers are split between a President and a Prime Minister.

FOCUS ON

Freedom of expression

Anti-blasphemy laws and defamation laws against public officials and Heads of State seriously restrict free speech. Some countries even regard blasphemy towards holy personages or the official religion as an offence punishable by death.

The extent to which freedom of opinion and expression can be restricted by a government is one of the most challenged and sensitive topics in international human rights law. Some countries continue to jail, torture and kill people who to speak out and express their views. The United Nations advocates for the protection of the right of all men, women and children to free expression.

United Nations officials help ellections in the Central African Republic.
Free elections are crucial for allowing all people to participate in making decisions
that affect them. ■ UN PHOTO/NEKTARIOS MARKOGIANNIS

What all democracies share and must respect is the freedom of their citizens and, most importantly for the democracy itself, the freedoms of expression, speech, association and the press, all essential for citizens to stay informed, make their voices heard and be able to vote according to their best interests. Also, key to the survival of the democratic system are respect for human rights and the holding of periodic and genuine multiparty elections by universal suffrage, which means including all men and women of eligible voting age.

Democracy provides a natural environment for the protection and effective realization of human rights. A democratic system empowers people to make decisions about their government, their lives and their future. It also fosters the development of individuals and communities who feel they can work to better their lives and, on a larger scale, improve society.

Overcoming Poverty

POVERTY AS A VIOLATION OF HUMAN RIGHTS

Poverty and human rights are intrinsically linked. Being out of work and therefore out of income is, of course, the basic definition of poverty, but to really understand what the condition is, one must also take into account a myriad of social, cultural and political factors. Poverty is not only a deprivation of economic or material resources; it is a violation of human rights, too.

Being poor often means being deprived of economic and social rights such as the rights to health care, adequate housing, food and safe water, education and work. Poor people are locked in a vicious cycle: without work, they have no money, so they can't pay for health services and food; sick and malnourished adults can't go to work, and their children can't go to school; but without an education, these children will not find work either. The same is true of civil and political rights, such as the rights to a fair trial, political participation and security of the person. Poor people feel that they have no voice, that no one hears them.

The pursuit of human rights promotes the freedom, dignity and worth of every person—so, too, does the pursuit of human development. The fundamental recognition of the human rights dimension of poverty is reshaping the United Nations approach to the next generation of poverty reduction initiatives and policies. Attention is now given to the critical vulnerability and daily assaults on human dignity that accompany poverty. Overcoming poverty is at the heart of the United Nations' Sustainable Development Goals.

ADDING A HUMAN RIGHTS DIMENSION TO DEVELOPMENT PROGRAMMES

To effectively eradicate poverty, the United Nations has added a human rights dimension to its development programmes. The pursuit of economic growth should not adversely affect the poor but, on the contrary, reinforce their ability to participate in the economic, political and social life of their societies by protecting their fundamental rights. Over the past decade, with this goal in mind, many countries have put in place or strengthened social protection initiatives to combat poverty. Even low-income countries can make significant progress on the Sustainable Development Goals with social protection initiatives.

THE MULTIPLYING EFFECT OF GENDER ISSUES

One way to make great strides against poverty and in the respect of human rights is to ensure gender equality. Poverty affects women and girls disproportionately: they are more at risk to be marginalized, isolated or victimized by violence and trafficking. Numerous studies have shown a positive link between improvement in women's access to health care, education and other social benefits and economic growth, increased income and overall progress in a country's living standards.

Given that gender inequality helps perpetuate poverty, effective development strategies must include the protection of the full range of women's rights. The eradication of poverty must be based on sustained economic growth, social development, environmental protection and social justice, and it requires equal opportunities and the full involvement of women.

COMBATING DISCRIMINATION AGAINST WOMEN

Gender equality is essential for the achievement of human rights for all, yet discriminatory laws against women persist in certain cultures. In some countries, laws continue to give women and girls second-class status with regard to na-

Educating women does not benefit just the students, but also their communities and society at large. A child born to an educated mother has much better chances of survival. ■ UN PHOTO/EVAN SCHNEIDER

tionality and citizenship, health, education, marital rights, employment rights, parental rights, inheritance and property rights. Such discrimination against women is incompatible with human rights.

Women form the majority of the world's poorest people, and the number of women living in rural poverty has increased by 50 per cent since 1975. Women labour for two thirds of the world's working hours and produce half of the world's food, yet they earn only 10 per cent of the world's income and own less than 1 per cent of the world's property.

Violence against women prevails on an unimaginable scale, and women's access to justice is often restricted. Discrimination based on gender and other factors, such as race, ethnicity, caste, disability, HIV/AIDS status or sexual orientation, further compounds the risk of economic hardship, exclusion and violence.

In some countries, women, unlike men, cannot dress as they like, drive, work at night, inherit property or give evidence in court. The majority of blatant discriminatory laws currently in force relate to family life, often limiting a woman's right to marry (or the right not to marry, in cases of early, forced marriages) or to divorce and remarry, thus allowing for sexually discriminatory marital practices like wife obedience and polygamy. Laws explicitly mandating "wife obedience" still govern marital relations in a number of countries.

International human rights law, in particular the Convention on the Elimination of All Forms of Discrimination against Women, prohibits gender discrimination and includes guarantees for men and women to enjoy their civil, cultural, economic, political and social rights equally.

Since the Convention's entry into force, the recognition and enjoyment of rights equal to those enjoyed by men still remain elusive for large populations of women around the world. By 2017, 189 States had ratified the Convention, yet some countries continue to discriminate against women in areas of personal and family life such as divorce, travel and education.

Combating discrimination against older people

The composition of the global population has changed dramatically in recent decades. Between 1950 and 2017 life expectancy worldwide rose from 46 to more than 71 years, and it is projected to increase to 81 by the end of the century. Almost 700 million people are now over the age of 60; by 2050, that number will reach 2 billion people, over 20 per cent of the global population and, for the first time in history, greater than the number of children in the world. Human rights don't stop at 60!

Clearly, we need to pay increased attention to the needs and challenges faced by older people. Just as important, however, are the essential contributions the majority of older men and women can continue to make to society if adequate guarantees are in place. Human rights lie at the core of all these efforts.

FOCUS ON

The United Nations wants to end violence against women

The United Nations UNiTE to End Violence against Women campaign aims to raise public awareness and increase political will and resources for preventing and ending all forms of violence against women and girls in all parts of the world.

UNiTE Goals

- Adoption and enforcement of national laws to address and punish all forms of violence against women and girls, in line with international human rights standards.

- Adoption and implementation of multisectoral national action plans that emphasize prevention and that are adequately resourced.

- Establishment of data collection and analysis systems on the prevalence of various forms of violence against women and girls.

- Establishment of national and/or local campaigns and the engagement of a diverse range of civil society actors in preventing violence and in supporting women and girls who have been abused.

- Systematic efforts to address sexual violence in conflict situations and to protect women and girls from rape as a tactic of war and full implementation of related laws and policies.

Building a just society for all women and girls and for all ages is part of the United Nations action to promote human rights across the globe. ■ UN PHOTO/KIM HAUGHTON

The Madrid International Plan of Action on Ageing and the Political Declaration adopted at the Second World Assembly on Ageing in April 2002 marked a turning point in how the world addresses the key challenge of "building a society for all ages". The Madrid Plan focuses on three priority areas: older persons and development, advancing health and well-being into old age and ensuring enabling and supportive environments. The Plan of Action is a resource for policymaking, suggesting ways for governments, non-governmental organizations and other actors to reorient the ways in which their societies perceive, interact with and care for older citizens. It represents the first time countries agreed to link questions of ageing to other frameworks for social and economic development and human rights.

COMBATING RACIAL DISCRIMINATION

Racial and ethnic discrimination occur on a daily basis, hindering progress for millions of people around the world. From denying individuals the basic principles of equality and non-discrimination to fuelling ethnic hatred that may lead to genocide, racism and intolerance destroy lives and communities. The struggle against racism is a matter of priority for the United Nations System.

The United Nations has been concerned with this issue since its founding, and the prohibition of racial discrimination is enshrined in all of the Organization's core international human rights instruments. The United Nations tasks States with eradicating discrimination in the public and private spheres. The principle of equality also requires States to adopt special measures to eliminate conditions that cause or perpetuate racial discrimination.

In 2001, the World Conference against Racism produced the most authoritative and comprehensive programme for combating racism, racial discrimination,

Indigenous peoples face many challenges in maintaining their identity, traditions and customs, and their cultural contributions are at times exploited and commercialized, with little or no recognition. ■ UN PHOTO/JOHN ISAAC

xenophobia and related intolerance: the Durban Declaration and Programme of Action. In April 2009, the Durban Review Conference examined global progress in overcoming racism and concluded that more remained to be achieved. The Conference renewed the world's commitment to an antiracism agenda.

COMBATING DISCRIMINATION AGAINST MINORITIES

Virtually all countries in the world have national, ethnic, linguistic and religious minorities within their borders. These groups and their members often face violations of their civil, cultural, economic, political and social rights on the basis of their defining characteristics.

FOCUS ON

Celebrating Nelson Mandela

The elimination of South Africa's system of legalized racial discrimination, known as *apartheid* ("apart-ness" in the Afrikaans language), was on the United Nations agenda from its inception.

Condemning apartheid as a crime against humanity, the United Nations carried out a sustained campaign against it for more than three decades. It assisted in and supervised the country's first free and multiracial elections in 1994. Nelson Mandela, who was jailed under apartheid, became the first President of racially integrated South Africa.

Nelson Mandela International Day is celebrated by the United Nations every year on 18 July (Mandela's birthday).

Minority issues have been on the agenda of the United Nations for more than 60 years. Already, in 1948 the General Assembly declared that the United Nations could not remain indifferent to the fate of minorities. The 2005 World Summit Outcome reaffirmed the importance of minority rights, stating that "the promotion and protection of the rights of persons belonging to national or ethnic, religious and linguistic minorities contribute to political and social stability and peace and enrich the cultural diversity and heritage of society".

The main point of reference for the rights of minorities is the United Nations Declaration on the Rights of Persons Belonging to National or Ethnic Religious and Linguistic Minorities (1992). It includes a list of rights to which people belonging to minority groups are entitled, including the right to enjoy their own culture, to profess and practice their own religion and to use their own language. The Declaration reaffirms that people belonging to minorities should enjoy all human rights in accordance with the principles of non-discrimination and equality before the law. Other key ideas include the protection of the existence and promotion of identity and the right to effective participation.

Combating discrimination against indigenous peoples

The world's indigenous population is estimated at 370 million individuals living in more than 70 countries and is made up of more than 5,000 distinct peoples. Although they represent 5 per cent of the world's population, indigenous peoples account for 15 per cent of its poorest people. They face many challenges, and their human rights are frequently violated: they are denied control over their own development based on their own values, needs and priorities,

The United Nations and the Holocaust

FOCUS ON

The Holocaust, which resulted in the murder of one third of the Jewish people along with countless members of other minorities, will forever be a warning to all people of the dangers of hatred, bigotry, racism and prejudice.

Rejecting any denial of the Holocaust as a historical event, either in full or in part, the United Nations General Assembly adopted by consensus a resolution condemning "without reserve" all manifestations of religious intolerance, incitement, harassment or violence against persons or communities based on ethnic origin or religious belief, whenever they occur.

The United Nations designated 27 January—the anniversary of the liberation of the Auschwitz Nazi death camp in 1945—as an annual International Day of Commemoration to honour the victims of the Holocaust. The Organization established an outreach programme, "The Holocaust and the United Nations," as well as measures to mobilize civil society for Holocaust remembrance and education, in order to help prevent the possibility of genocide occurring ever again.

and they are politically underrepresented and lack access to social and other services. They are often marginalized in discussions of projects affecting their lands and have been the victims of forced displacement as a result of ventures involving the exploitation of natural resources.

In 2007, the General Assembly adopted the United Nations Declaration on the Indigenous Peoples, following more than two decades of negotiations between governments and indigenous peoples' representatives.

The Declaration is a key tool for the promotion and protection of the rights of indigenous peoples. It establishes a universal framework of minimum standards for survival, dignity, well-being and rights. It addresses individual and collective rights, cultural rights and identity and rights to education, health, employment and language. It outlaws discrimination against indigenous peoples and promotes their full and effective participation in all matters that concern them. The Declaration also ensures the rights of indigenous peoples to remain distinct and pursue their own priorities in economic, social and cultural development.

COMBATING DISCRIMINATION AGAINST MIGRANTS

The Durban Declaration, adopted by the World Conference against Racism in 2001, pointed out that xenophobia against non-nationals, in particular migrants, constitutes one of the main sources of contemporary racism. Migrants are often discriminated against in housing, education, health care, work and social security. This is a global issue affecting the countries of origin, countries of transit and countries of arrival. Around 244 million people lived outside their countries of origin in 2015 and the trend has dramatically increased since then.

Migrants arriving illegally in a new country and victims of trafficking stopped by the police are often detained in administrative centres or prisons. Although the deprivation of liberty should be a last resort under international human rights law, migrants are often detained as a routine procedure and without proper judicial safeguards. Overcrowded immigration detention centres often have poor access to health care and inadequate food, sanitation or safe drinking water. There is also an increasing tendency to criminalize migration, which has, in too many cases, resulted in violations of migrants' rights.

Addressing negative perceptions of migrants within host communities is a key element of promoting their integration and enhancing their contribution to development. Various United Nations instruments, in particular the International Convention on the Protection of the Rights of All Migrant Workers and Members of their Families, address the issue of discrimination and provide guidance on human rights safeguards.

COMBATING DISCRIMINATION AGAINST PERSONS WITH DISABILITIES

One billion people around the world live with disabilities. That is 15 per cent of the world's population in 2017. In every country, people with disabilities often live on the margins of society, deprived of some of life's fundamental experi-

Children whose rights are respected are happier and healthier. ■ UN PHOTO/STEPHANIE HOLLYMAN

ences. They have little hope of going to school, getting a job, having their own home, starting a family and raising children, socializing or voting.

Persons with disabilities make up the world's largest and most disadvantaged minority. Around a third of the world's street children live with disabilities, and the literacy rate for adults with disabilities is as low as three per cent.

The Convention on the Rights of Persons with Disabilities is the United Nation's response to the long history of discrimination, exclusion and dehumanization of this marginalized group. A record number of countries have signed the Convention and its Protocol.

CHILDREN TOO HAVE RIGHTS

Human rights apply to all age groups: children have the same human rights as adults. But children are particularly vulnerable, and so they also have special rights that recognize their need for protection.

Providing legal protection for children

Convention on the Rights of the Child

The Convention on the Rights of the Child sets out the rights that must be realized for children to develop their full potential, free from hunger and want, neglect and abuse. Children are neither the property of their parents nor are they helpless objects of charity. They are human beings with their own rights. The Convention offers a vision of the child as an individual and as a member of a family and community, with rights and responsibilities appropriate to his or her age and stage of development.

This United Nations Convention, a universally agreed-upon set of non-negotiable standards and obligations, has heightened recognition of the fundamental human dignity of children and the urgency of ensuring their well-being and development. It makes clear that an essential quality of life should be the right of all children, rather than a privilege enjoyed by only a few.

Optional Protocols to the Convention

In adopting the Convention, the international community recognized that people under 18 years of age need special care and protection. To help stem the growing abuse and exploitation of children worldwide, the General Assembly adopted two Optional Protocols to the Convention, to increase the protection of children from involvement in armed conflicts and from sexual exploitation:

- The Optional Protocol on the involvement of children in armed conflict establishes 18 as the minimum age for compulsory recruitment and requires States to do everything they can to prevent individuals under the age of 18 from taking a direct part in hostilities.

- The Optional Protocol on the sale of children, child prostitution and child pornography draws special attention to the criminalization of these serious violations of children's rights. It aims to increase public awareness and cooperation between countries in efforts to combat them.

Children's rights

Definition of a child

The Convention defines a child as a person below the age of 18, unless the laws of a particular country set the legal age for adulthood younger. The Committee on the Rights of the Child, the monitoring body for the Convention, has encouraged States to review the age of majority if it is set below 18 and to increase the level of protection for all children under 18.

DID YOU KNOW

An optional protocol is a treaty related to a main convention

Very often, human rights treaties such as the Convention on the Rights of the Child are followed by Optional Protocols, which may either provide procedures regarding the treaty in question or address a substantive area related to that treaty.

Optional Protocols to human rights treaties are treaties in their own right and are open to signature, accession or ratification by countries that are party to the main "parent" treaty.

Responsibilities and obligations

Parents, either natural or adoptive—or in some instances legal guardians, have the primary responsibility to provide for, protect and raise their children. However, governments of countries that have ratified the Convention are obligated to ensure that the children's rights are respected, protected and fulfilled. This involves assessing their social services and legal, health and educational systems, as well as levels of funding for these services. They must help families protect children's rights and create an environment where kids can grow and reach their potential. Governments should make the Convention known to adults and children. All adults, primarily parents and teachers, should help children learn about their rights, too.

What are children's rights?

Every child has the right to:

- Life.

- A legally registered name.

- A nationality.

- An identity (an official record of who they are).

- Care and guidance by both parents, unless they represent a threat to the well-being of the child, or if they become separated from the child, in which case a legal guardian assumes the parenting role.

- Direct contact with both parents, in case of separation from one or both parents, except if it is contrary to the child's best interests.

- Crossing borders to visit or be reunited with family living in other countries.

- Protection from all forms of physical or mental violence, injury or abuse, neglect, maltreatment or exploitation, including sexual abuse, discrimination, abduction, sale and trafficking.

- Appropriate protection and care (special attention must be given to the most vulnerable, like refugee children or those with disabilities).

- Freedom of speech, thought and religion.

- Freedom of association.

- Privacy.

- Information (on his or her environment and rights, health issues and more).

- Participation in decisions affecting him or her.

- An adequate standard of living to meet physical and mental needs.

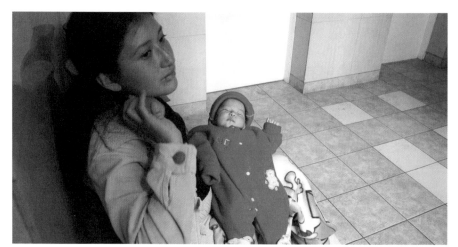

The first right of every child is the right to life. Parents or legal guardians have the primary responsibility to provide for, protect and raise their children. ■ UNFPA PHOTO/CARINA WINT

- The best health care possible, safe drinking water, nutritious food and a clean and safe environment.

- Help from the government if he or she is poor or in need, particularly with regard to food, clothing and housing.

- A primary education, which should be free, in order to develop each child's personality, talents and abilities to the fullest and to learn respect for peace and others' rights.

- Leisure, play and culture.

- Protection against work that is dangerous, inappropriate for children or that jeopardizes his or her other rights (health, education, leisure).

- A fair juvenile justice system, protecting detained children from abuse and treating them with dignity.

- Freedom from torture or cruel, inhuman or degrading treatment.

- Protection from the consequences of war and armed conflicts and especially from recruitment by armed forces.

- Rehabilitation if he or she has been neglected, abused or exploited, with special attention to restoring a child's health, self-respect and dignity.

The United Nations and children's rights

The United Nations and its agencies are involved at all levels in upholding and applying children's rights, offering a forum for States to discuss related issues, as well as direct services for children on the ground and around the world.

From vaccination campaigns to provision of clean water and sanitation services, from the protection of child refugees to the rehabilitation of former child soldiers and victims of armed conflicts, the United Nations System is improving children's lives every day, working to make the world a better and safer place for them.

Education for all children

The Education for All movement, a global commitment to providing quality basic education for all children, teenagers and adults, was launched at the landmark World Conference on Education for All in 1990. Since then, great progress has been achieved. By 2015, enrolment in primary education in developing countries had reached 91 per cent, but 57 million children remain out of school today.

Obtaining a quality education is the foundation to improving people's lives and sustainable development. Major progress has been made towards increasing access to education at all levels and increasing enrolment rates in schools, particularly for women and girls. Basic literacy skills have improved tremendously, yet bolder efforts are needed to make even greater strides for achieving universal education goals. For example, the world has achieved equality in primary education between girls and boys, but few countries have achieved that target at all levels of education.

Among its many targets, **Sustainable Development Goal number four (SDG 4)** aims to ensure that by 2030:

- All girls and boys complete free, equitable and quality primary and secondary education.
- All girls and boys have access to quality early childhood development, care and preprimary education.
- All women and men have access to affordable and quality technical, vocational and tertiary education, including university.

FOCUS ON

Children and justice systems

Over one million children are estimated to be detained worldwide. Most of them have not committed serious offences. In many cases children are detained for political reasons and have committed no crime at all.

Prison conditions in many countries, particularly those affected by conflict and crisis, are dire in terms of disease, sanitation and the need for water and food. The lack of access to education, health care or family members for long periods of time affects all prisoners, especially children. Inhumane conditions often lead to deaths and jeopardize the chances of a prisoner's social reintegration.

Offering a free meal to schoolchildren encourages enrolment and attendance, and increases students' learning capacity. ■ UN PHOTO/MARTINE PERRET

SENDING GIRLS TO SCHOOL

Thanks in large part to the United Nations, today more than 90 per cent of primary-school-age children are enrolled in school, a big jump from less than 50 per cent in 1960. This is great progress, but a lot remains to be done.

In some developing countries, girls were still facing discrimination in 2017. They often receive less food than boys do and are forced to work long hours, even when they are only five or six years old.

The Convention on the Rights of the Child requires governments to ensure that both girls and boys get an education. The obstacles that stand between girls and schooling are mainly due to poverty, armed conflict, cultural and religious mores and geography.

Educating a girl dramatically reduces the chances that any children she has will die before age five. Educated girls are likely to marry later and have fewer children, who in turn will be more likely to survive and be educated. Educated girls are more productive at home, better paid in the workplace and more able to participate in decision-making, which in turn makes countries more prosperous, in line with the United Nations Sustainable Development Goals.

Child labour

All over the world today, millions of children work to help their families in ways that are neither harmful nor exploitative. However, 168 million children remain

Child labour is prevalent in all parts of the world. ■ UN PHOTO/JEAN PIERRE LAFONT

trapped in child labour. Over half of them are exposed to hazardous environments, slavery, prostitution, drug trafficking, armed conflict and other illicit activities.

Child labour is both a cause and a consequence of poverty and is a violation of human rights. It harms the children, their families and their communities. It also prevents countries from making progress towards their development. Child labour is deeply linked to social inequities reinforced by discrimination. Children from indigenous groups, minorities, lower castes and of migrants are more likely not to attend school.

There has been considerable progress in the ratification of the International Labour Organization's (ILO) standards concerning child labour, namely of conventions on the worst forms of such labour and on minimum working age. However, a third of the world's children live in countries that have not yet ratified these conventions. Under the lead of the ILO, the United Nations is committed to achieving the elimination of the worst forms of child labour.

Fighting child selection

The Office of the High Commissioner for Human Rights (OHCHR), the United Nations Population Fund (UNFPA), the United Nations Children Fund (UNICEF), UN-Women and the World Health Organization (WHO) work against sex selection, a process favouring boys that takes place in some parts of the world, where ratios as high as 130 boys for every 100 girls have been observed. Sex selection is a symptom of social, cultural, political and economic injustices against

All children, boys and girls, have the same rights. ■ UN PHOTO/ESKINDER DEBEBE

women, and a manifest violation of human rights. Some parents often seek to discover the sex of a foetus through ultrasound, which can lead to abortion.

In some countries, prenatal sex determination and disclosure are illegal, while others have laws banning abortion for sex selection. But such restrictions are circumvented by clandestine procedures which jeopardize women's health. In some areas, the lack of women has become so acute that it has led to an upsurge in their trafficking from other regions. States are obliged to act against these human rights violations.

In March 2017, UNFPA, with funding from the European Union, launched the Global Programme to Prevent Son Preference and Gender-Biased Sex Selection. The programme works with governments and local partners to gather data about unequal sex ratios at birth in Asia and the Caucasus with a view to design human rights-based and gender-equality focused interventions.

Chapter 6

HUMANITARIAN CRISES
AND RESPONSES

QUICK FACTS ABOUT HUMANITARIAN CRISES AND RESPONSES

- When an event (or a series of events) critically threatens the health, safety, security or well-being of a large group of people, usually over a wide area, it is called a **humanitarian crisis or disaster.**

- **Wars, violence, epidemics, famines, natural disasters** and other emergencies may all involve or lead to humanitarian crises.

- Nearly 90 per cent of natural disasters today are caused by **climate** and **water-related hazards** such as floods, tropical storms and long periods of drought.

- There have been 6,457 **weather-related disasters** between 1995 and 2015, and there has been a doubling of such events yearly over the last decade.

- In 2015, the number of ongoing **armed conflicts** increased to 50 compared to 41 in 2014.

- Four **disasters** killed more than 1,000 people in 2015: the Gorkha **earthquake** in Nepal of April (8,831 deaths) and three **heat waves**: in France between June and August (3,275 deaths), in India in May (2,248 deaths) and in Pakistan in June (1,229 deaths).

- The aggregate economic and financial **cost of conflict** in 2014 was estimated to be $14.3 billion, or 13.4 per cent of the global economy

- Over the last decade, China, the United States, India, the Philippines and Indonesia constituted together the **top five countries** that are most frequently hit by **natural disasters**.

- In 2017, An unprecedented **65.6 million** people around the world have been forced from home. Among them are nearly **22.5 million refugees**, over half of whom are under the age of 18.

- Many countries and subnational areas now face cycles of repeated **violence**, weak governance, and instability.

- Most **armed conflicts** today happen within countries and not between countries.

Different types of disasters

Natural disasters

Every year, more than 200 million people are affected by natural disasters. Weather, climate and water-related hazards such as floods, tropical storms and long periods of drought account for nearly 90 per cent of natural disasters today. They destroy countless lives, leaving many people homeless and displaced. Sometimes they destroy livelihoods and community infrastructures, as when they render roads inaccessible and kill off resources necessary for the next harvest. Significant food shortage and the spread of infections and diseases can also create chronic crises and emergencies in the aftermath of a natural disaster.

Man-made disasters

Another type of disaster is human-caused, triggered by conflicts or civil wars. Man-made disasters uproot millions of people across the globe, leading to a wide range of emergencies, including food crises and massive displacement of populations. Victims of man-made disasters are usually forced to leave their homes and live on the edge, eking out an existence without the protection of their basic rights. During exile, many are exposed to violence, abuse or exploitation. They may have difficulty gaining access to facilities that secure safe water, as wells are often contaminated or mined by combatants during a conflict. Hunger and malnutrition, loss of safety and security and poor access to basic services, especially health care, are a few examples of hardships triggered by man-made disasters.

Aftermath of a hurricane in Haiti. ■ UN/MINUSTAH PHOTO/LOGAN ABASSI

Recent disaster trends

In recent years, the trends in emergencies and crises have differed from the previous few decades, posing new threats and concerns to the world's population with highly complex and challenging issues. Those issues include a global food crisis, climate change and disease epidemics such as HIV/AIDS and Ebola.

In addition, the magnitude and frequency of disasters vary, and multiple disasters can occur simultaneously. A recent trend shows a series of catastrophic natural and climate-related events that have required very high and sustained levels of humanitarian assistance from the international community and particularly from the United Nations.

DID YOU KNOW

Recent humanitarian crises

Recent available figures from the United Nations International Strategy for Disaster Reduction (UNISDR) show that between 1980 and 2012, 42 million life years were lost in internationally reported disasters. The concept of "human life years" provides a better representation of disaster impact, as it provides a metric describing the time required to produce economic development and social progress.

Over 80 per cent were spread across low and middle-income countries, representing a serious setback to social and economic development.

The Middle East and Northern Africa: A wave of political turmoil has swept the region since 2011 and caused widespread violence across Libya, Syria, Yemen and other States in the region. An estimated 5.5 million Syrians were forced to seek refuge abroad, and about two million people have been displaced because of the war in Yemen.

In 2017, the world faced the largest humanitarian crisis since the Second World War, with more than 20 million people facing starvation in Yemen, South Sudan, Somalia and northeast Nigeria.

The Nepal Earthquake: In April 2015, a deadly earthquake shook the nation of Nepal to its very foundations, killing an estimated 9,000 people and razing much of its infrastructure and world-renowned historic sites to the ground, with dire consequences for its people, economy and tourism industry.

The conflict in Eastern Europe: In Ukraine, more than 10,000 people have been killed, and an estimated 1.7 million people have been displaced, many of them children, since the beginning of the conflict that followed the invasion of Crimea in 2014 and outbreak of hostilities in the Donbas region. The infrastructure of the region has been completely destroyed, causing widespread economic and social pain for the local populations as well as renewed East/West tensions.

The Zaatri Refugee Camp in Jordan. ■ UN PHOTO/MARK GARTEN

The impact of disasters: key humanitarian needs and risk management

Food

Food is our most basic human need, and it is also a human right. An empty stomach slows down physical and mental activities. With a lack of vital nutrients in the system, the hungry body has difficulty fighting against disease and infection. Today, hunger and malnutrition constitute the number one health risk worldwide, claiming millions of lives.

Shelter

The idea of shelter, or home, represents peace and comfort, protection and security. Home is a place where we live, play, eat, sleep and rest. People who lose their shelter and live in precarious conditions, with no access to basic needs, can experience severe stress and emotional discomfort. Having a home is vital for survival, which is why all human beings have the right to housing as part of an adequate standard of living.

Water, sanitation and hygiene

Lack of access to safe water and sanitation facilities, as well as poor hygienic practices, can cause major health problems. Dirty hands and dirty water allow viruses and bacteria to spread easily. Millions of people, especially children in developing countries, suffer from water- and sanitation-related diseases and infections, including gastroenteritis, cholera, malaria, parasites and worm infestations. The right to live in healthy conditions is guaranteed under international standards.

Education

In school, children and adolescents learn academic, vocational and life skills. School provides a safe environment where they can play and interact with peers, reducing the possible risk of their exposure to violence. The right of children to benefit from education is also guaranteed under international standards.

One of the largest airplanes in the world, the Ukrainian-designed Antonov 124, can carry a helicopter across the globe in minimal time and has been heavily used by the United Nations for relief operations. ■ UN PHOTO/ARI GAITANIS

Coordination of emergency assistance

For successful delivery of emergency relief action, it is crucial to have an accurate assessment of the situation at the onset of a crisis. This includes a breakdown of exactly what kind of humanitarian assistance is most needed, who will be the beneficiaries of such assistance, how long such aid will be provided for and what kind of logistical difficulties will most likely be encountered.

There are many actors involved in humanitarian action—the United Nations System, governments, NGOs, civil society, local and international partners and many other relief agencies. Together they constitute the backbone of the international humanitarian community, working to feed the hungry, relieve the poor and provide shelter, protection and care to those who have lost their homes and family members. Only through an effective partnership and coordination among these actors is it possible to achieve success in humanitarian work.

Inter-agency coordination

As the Secretariat of the Inter-Agency Standing Committee (IASC) and of rapid-response teams, the United Nations Office for the Coordination of Humanitarian Affairs (OCHA) plays a crucial role in the immediate assessment of a humanitarian crisis and coordination of joint assistance. It can dispatch the United Nations Disaster Assessment and Coordination (UNDAC) team within 48 hours of a crisis anywhere in the world.

OCHA has adopted IASC's "cluster approach" in the coordination of pro-grammes. This groups together United Nations and non-United Nations hu-manitarian agencies with a shared operational interest and divides field re-sponsibilities among them. The "cluster approach" is effective in helping agencies avoid gaps and duplications in their humanitarian roles and under-take relief activities to the best of their capabilities.

In responding to disasters, the clusters cover a wide range of areas—agriculture, camp coordination and management, early recovery, emergency shelter, logis-tics, nutrition, water sanitation and hygiene, restoration of telecommunications, and more. The Office of the United Nations High Commissioner for Refugees/the United Nations Refugee Agency (UNHCR) is a global leader for emergency shelter cluster. When there is a massive influx of refugees or internally dis-placed persons (IDPs) in a region, UNHCR will put together all of the available assistance from many humanitarian partners and lead the relief action to pro-vide refugees and IDPs with temporary shelter and other basic supplies.

Who are the humanitarian workers?

The humanitarian workers are doctors and surgeons, nurses, psychologists, teachers, photographers, journalists, TV and radio technicians, car and lorry drivers, plane and helicopter pilots, economists, auditors, jurists, press of-ficers, translators and interpreters. They are experts in fields as diverse as agriculture, communication, human rights, climate change, water resource management, accounting, finance, logistics, disaster prevention, democratic governance, terrorism and engineering. They are specialists in nutrition, gen-

World Food Programme emergency food relief in South Sudan. ◼ UN PHOTO/ISAAC BILLY

der issues, multimedia, education, information technologies, sanitation services, police training, rebuilding of livelihoods and post-traumatic therapy. They are administrators, coordinators, project managers, advisers, employees, consultants, volunteers and people from local communities, all highly dedicated men and women from around the world.

Despite these many differences, they have a lot in common. Humanitarian workers dedicate themselves to assisting those in need, regardless of the recipients' race, religion or social status. They operate in places that are often remote, difficult and hostile. They risk their own lives to help others. Many have lost colleagues or loved ones as, over the years, humanitarian work has become more dangerous. The level of threats and number of deliberate attacks on aid organizations, including staff, equipment and facilities, has risen dramatically in recent years.

UNITED NATIONS AGENCIES IN THE FIELD: WHO IS ON THE GROUND?

Immediate emergency response: saving more lives

Immediate emergency response covers most crises that require instantaneous relief action, ranging from slow-onset hazards like droughts or crop failures to more complex disasters involving armed conflict or population displacement. In the field, United Nations agencies and many other humanitarian organizations work around the clock to meet the most critical needs during crises. Some high-profile emergencies require a concerted action involving various humanitarian bodies for a longer period of time, depending on scope and scale.

World Food Programme (WFP)

- **What it does:** Feeds the hungry and poor.

- **How it operates:** Establishes an emergency operation within 24 hours of a disaster outbreak to feed survivors.

The World Food Programme (WFP) procures locally produced food to cut down on transportation costs and help sustain local economies. Half of the food distributed by WFP is procured within the affected country or near crisis zones.

Food is given to the hungry at refugee camps, therapeutic feeding centres and other emergency shelters.

World Health Organization (WHO)

- **What it does:** Fights against outbreaks of emerging epidemic-prone diseases.

- **How it operates:** Distributes emergency vaccines and supplies for local health facilities during crises.

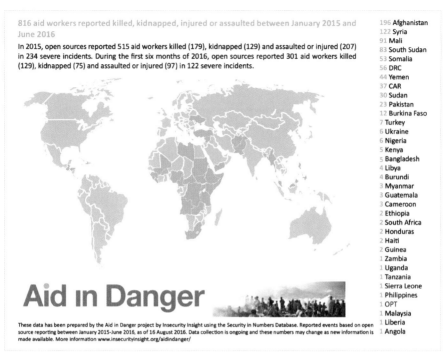

816 aid workers reported killed, kidnapped, injured or assaulted between January 2015 and June 2016

In 2015, open sources reported 515 aid workers killed (179), kidnapped (129) and assaulted or injured (207) in 234 severe incidents. During the first six months of 2016, open sources reported 301 aid workers killed (129), kidnapped (75) and assaulted or injured (97) in 122 severe incidents.

196 Afghanistan
122 Syria
91 Mali
83 South Sudan
53 Somalia
56 DRC
44 Yemen
37 CAR
30 Sudan
23 Pakistan
12 Burkina Faso
7 Turkey
6 Ukraine
6 Nigeria
5 Kenya
5 Bangladesh
4 Libya
4 Burundi
3 Myanmar
3 Guatemala
3 Cameroon
2 Ethiopia
2 South Africa
2 Honduras
2 Haiti
2 Guinea
1 Zambia
1 Uganda
1 Tanzania
1 Sierra Leone
1 Philippines
1 OPT
1 Malaysia
1 Liberia
1 Angola

Aid in Danger

These data has been prepared by the Aid in Danger project by Insecurity Insight using the Security In Numbers Database. Reported events based on open source reporting between January 2015-June 2016, as of 16 August 2016. Data collection is ongoing and these numbers may change as new information is made available. More information www.insecurityinsight.org/aidindanger/

Source: http://reliefweb.int/report/world/aid-danger-aid-workers-reported-killed-kid-napped-injured-or-assaulted-between-january

The World Health Organization (WHO) treats communicable diseases, including HIV/AIDS, tuberculosis, malaria, measles and influenza in affected communities.

United Nations Children's Fund (UNICEF)

- **What it does**: Child survival and protection, development and education.

- **How it operates:** UNICEF's Supply Division can pack and ship essential emergency supplies and pre-packaged kits within 48 hours following a disaster.

UNICEF provides emergency immunization, vitamin A supplementation and other health services for children and their families. It also provides basic care services for HIV/AIDS and post-rape and psychosocial health training for community health-care workers.

For water, sanitation and hygiene crises, it rehabilitates water points and constructs hand-washing facilities and latrines.

It operates therapeutic feeding centres and supports local schools in reconstructing classrooms for children.

*Young refugee girl with a food ration in a temporary
United Nations housing facility.* ■ UN PHOTO/JOHN ISAAC

Examples of field actions in 2017

■ **WFP** provided immediate relief to victims of the Myanmar crisis.

WFP distributed food to people fleeing into Bangladesh to escape violence in Myanmar's Rakhine State in 2017. An estimated 146,000 people had streamed across the border into the district of Cox's Bazar in the summer of 2017 alone.

■ **WHO** launched a vaccination campaign in the Horn of Africa.

WHO urgently mobilized funds to scale up its response activities in Somalia and conduct a measles immunization campaign for 4.2 million children in November 2017.

■ **UNICEF** is helping children all over the world.

In 2017, in Syria alone, UNICEF aimed to reach out to 2.5 million individuals with mine risk education activities. UNICEF provided for 320,000 children and adults participating in structured and sustained child-protection programmes.

■ Recent **UNHCR** relief response in the Mediterranean.

During 2017, UNHCR responded to the emergency caused by Syrians fleeing their country for Europe by mobilizing over 600 staff and resources in 20 different locations to provide life-saving assistance and protection.

Office of the United Nations High Commissioner for Refugees/The United Nations Refugee Agency (UNHCR)

- **What it does:** Assists and protects forcibly displaced people.

- **Who it helps:** Refugees, asylum seekers, returnees, internally displaced people, stateless people and others in similar situations, children and women in particular.

- **How it operates:** UNHCR can dispatch 300 skilled personnel in less than 72 hours following a crisis.

UNHCR provides emergency shelter—refugee camps, collective centres, makeshift shelters—and essential goods, including tents, blankets and plastic sheeting. It helps build clinics, schools and water wells for shelter inhabitants and gives them access to health care and psychosocial support during their exile. It coordinates family reunification activities and demobilization, disarmament and integration programmes for children associated with armed forces.

FOCUS ON

Children during crises

Children are especially vulnerable during emergencies. Each year, almost 11 million children die before reaching the age of five. More than two million children died from armed conflict in the last decade, and more than 20 million children were displaced worldwide, while about 300,000 under the age of 18 were recruited as war soldiers.

Children can easily become victims of:

- Extreme poverty.

- Hunger and malnutrition, which weaken a child's learning ability and affect the immune system. When a woman suffers from malnutrition during pregnancy, her baby is at risk of being born with a low birth weight, which increases the risk of other health problems, disabilities or death.

- Infections or diseases: measles, diarrhoea, parasite or acute respiratory infections, malaria, HIV/AIDS.

- Severe injuries or death during emergencies.

- Unnecessary displacement or becoming orphaned during exile.

- Violence: abuse, exploitation, abduction, recruitment into armed conflict and sexual or gender-based violence (SGBV), including rape, prostitution, mutilation, forced pregnancy and sexual slavery.

Long-term emergency response: getting people back on their feet

From time to time, depending on the impact of a disaster or prolonged conflict, circumstances may require going beyond a one-time emergency response. In such cases, United Nations agencies, together with other humanitarian bodies, draw up long-term plans for recovery that entail complex and prolonged projects aiming to rebuild and develop the sustainability of crisis-ridden areas. Key focus activities during long-term emergency responses are:

- Increasing food security through continuous food assistance and introduction of new agricultural practices.
- Coordination of voluntary repatriation, resettlement or integration of refugees.
- Improvement of health-care services and community interventions.
- Securing safe water and improved sanitation facilities.
- Support for the education of children and teenagers.

United Nations Food and Agriculture Organization (FAO)

The United Nations Food and Agriculture Organization (FAO) aims to improve agricultural productivity in food-crisis regions. While continuing its food aid, it reaches out to rural populations in particular to help them rehabilitate their land and livelihoods and improve agricultural practices for food production security.

Long-term relief actions include the provision of drought-resistant seeds and fertilizers, fishing equipment, livestock and farm tools. With its expertise in farming, livestock, fisheries and forestry, FAO also provides information on rehabilitation, local food security and agricultural needs.

FAO's Special Programme for Food Security (SPFS) targets small-scale farmers by implementing low-cost technologies to increase profits, food and livestock production. The programme introduces improved breeds and high-value crops like rice, maize and onions as sources of farmers' income.

FAO also helps rehabilitate dams and introduces low-cost equipment (pedal or motorized pumps) for a consistent supply of water for food production.

FOCUS ON

Displaced men and boys

In an effort to ensure the protection of women and girls, discussions about humanitarian assistance have sometimes neglected the situation of adult men and young boys. They, too, have specific needs, face difficult situations and fear for their lives, survival and freedom. When refugee movements are provoked by a human-made disaster, like armed conflict—rather than a natural catastrophe, such as flooding—men and boys are often more directly affected. They run the risk of being forcibly recruited into armies and militia groups.

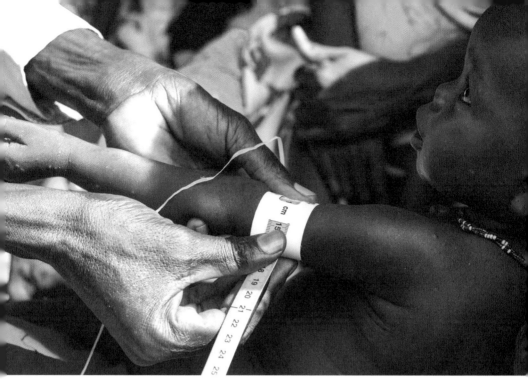

UNICEF and WFP launch joint nutrition response plan for South Sudan. ■ UN PHOTO/JC MCILWAINE

World Food Programme (WFP)

The World Food Programme (WFP)'s Protracted Relief and Recovery Operations (PRROs) facilitate the transition from relief to recovery in a wide range of areas, from education to community infrastructure to food assistance.

The School Meals programme promises a nutritious meal—a mid-morning snack or breakfast—to children who attend school. Not only does the scheme provide vital nourishment for hungry children, but it also keeps them at school, where they learn essential skills in a safe environment. WFP's "take-home rations" project is especially designed to encourage education for young girls by providing a sack of rice and a can of cooking oil to families who send their daughters to school.

WFP also operates cash-for-work and food-for-work programmes in rural areas to help inhabitants generate income by participating in the resilience-building effort.

United Nations Children's Fund (UNICEF)

The United Nations Children's Fund (UNICEF)'s primary goal is to rebuild a protective and healthy environment for children and their families. In response to emergencies that require a long-term relief response, UNICEF covers areas that directly affect the health and well-being of children.

Through UNICEF's Back to School Campaigns, children participate in peace-building efforts and demobilization programmes, and learn how to support community reconciliation. UNICEF also organizes tracing and family reunification programmes for children who are displaced or orphaned.

World Health Organization (WHO)

The World Health Organization (WHO) promotes health and sponsors prevention and education activities for a variety of population groups. The long-term response activities of WHO include reconstructing housing with improved local drainage and built-in roof catchment systems, rebuilding markets with adequate hygienic facilities and repairing and deepening rural wells and boreholes.

Office of the United Nations High Commissioner for Refugees /the United Nations Refugee Agency (UNHCR)

During or after major refugee crises, the Office of the United Nations High Commissioner for Refugees (UNHCR) helps refugees and other forcibly displaced persons rebuild their lives in peace and dignity.

A refugee's voluntary repatriation to her or his country or region of origin is considered the most successful outcome of all. Upon a refugee's return home, UNHCR organizes "go-and-see" follow-up visits and provides safety information while engaging in community reconciliation activities and providing legal aid.

Refugees who cannot return home often integrate into host societies or resettle in a third country. In such cases, UNHCR supports integration programmes, such as cultural orientation, language and vocational training, and offers legal advice as well as psychological support to ensure that people are well integrated.

Emergency preparedness and prevention

Nothing is better than prevention. Although some natural or man-made disasters are difficult to predict, it is possible to reduce the risks from recurring disasters and prepare in advance in regions that are particularly prone to such extreme events. With the right preparedness, many more lives can be saved with much less effort. Before short-term or long-term relief efforts are even needed, United Nations agencies work with governments and other humanitarian organizations to prepare for and build resilience against future crises.

Improving living conditions

One such effort is to break the trap of poverty and hunger. The World Food Programme (WFP) and the United Nations Food and Agriculture Organization (FAO) provide information on world food security problems, including weather conditions for agriculture and crop prospects. FAO's Global Information and Early Warning System (GIEWS) provides early warnings of food crises, and its Emergency Prevention System (EMPRES) helps to protect the entire food chain against the spread of animal and plant disease. As an effort to increase food security and agriculture in local communities, the FAO assists in the construction of agricultural infrastructure, including roads, warehouses and irrigation. The United Nations Development Programme (UNDP) also participates in the construction of community infrastructure to help prevent future crises, for instance the rehabilitation of watersheds to reduce the risk of floods in regions particularly prone to them.

Reducing the impact of disasters

The United Nations International Strategy for Disaster Reduction (UNISDR) coordinates risk reduction activities and proposes strategic ways to reduce the impact of natural hazards. Its priorities are mainly directed to developing countries, where 85 per cent of the populations are exposed to natural disasters. UNISDR organizes and participates in various disaster risk reduction events around the world. It works with local communities, other international organizations, non-governmental organizations, private enterprises, governments and other stakeholders to raise awareness of dangers, encourage preparedness, and foster resilience in areas that are at risk.

The United Nations Children's Fund (UNICEF) has various ongoing prevention programmes, including an HIV/AIDS campaign that focuses on the prevention of mother-to-child transmission and HIV infection among teenagers and young people. UNICEF provides preventive treatment, reproductive health services, childbirth care and pediatric HIV care, counseling and psychological support for those who are affected, as well as information on HIV prevention and testing for young people in high-risk communities. The World Health Organization

FOCUS ON

People of concern: forcibly displaced persons

- **Refugees:** A refugee is someone who fled his or her home and country owing to "a well- founded fear of persecution because of his/her race, religion, nationality, membership in a particular social group, or political opinion", according to the United Nations 1951 Refugee Convention. Many refugees are in exile to escape the effects of natural or man-made disasters.

- **Asylum seeker:** Asylum seekers say they are refugees and have fled their homes as refugees do, but their claim to refugee status is not yet definitively evaluated in the country to which they fled.

- **Internally displaced persons (IDPs):** IDPs are people who have not crossed an international border but have moved to a different region than the one they call home within their own country.

- **Stateless persons:** Stateless persons do not have a recognized nationality and do not belong to any country. Statelessness situations are usually caused by discrimination against certain groups. Their lack of identification—a citizenship certificate—can exclude them from access to important government services, including health care, education or employment.

- **Returnees:** Returnees are former refugees who return to their own countries or regions of origin after time in exile. Returnees need continuous support and reintegration assistance to ensure that they can rebuild their lives at home.

The Secretary-General visits Antigua and Barbuda to survey hurricane damage in 2017. ◼ UN PHOTO/RICK BARJONAS

(WHO) also works to reduce high-risk factors that lead to health-related emergencies by supporting prevention campaigns and helping communities develop and improve essential health-care plans.

Humanitarian action for economic and social development

Many of the United Nations agencies' preparedness and prevention programmes directly address the United Nations Sustainable Development Goals—for instance, to halve hunger and poverty, achieve universal primary education and gender parity in education and combat HIV/AIDS by the end of 2030—all with the ultimate goal of overcoming the world's epidemic emergencies and crises.

FOCUS ON

The Horn of Africa: hunger and malnutrition

The people in the Horn of Africa have struggled against food and nutrition crises brought about by a devastating drought for decades.

Malnutrition and mortality rates are alarmingly high in the region. The estimated number of people needing food and other basic humanitarian services stands in the millions in Djibouti, Ethiopia, Kenya, Somalia and Uganda.

Conflict-ridden Somalia is one of the countries worst affected by this severe drought. The United Nations Food and Agriculture Organization (FAO) has issued agricultural recovery actions across the Horn of Africa to help save more lives and livelihoods in drought-struck regions. Its interventions include distribution of seeds, livestock vaccination and treatment and cash-for-work programmes.

FREQUENTLY ASKED QUESTIONS

Can individuals join the United Nations as members?

No, only independent countries with international recognition from other States can become members of the United Nations.

How can individuals support the United Nations?

Individuals can support the work of the United Nations through international and local non-governmental organizations (NGOs). Some of them collaborate with the United Nations Department of Public Information and provide the United Nations with valuable links to people around the world.

United Nations Associations

There are United Nations Associations in more than 100 countries, often with many local chapters (e.g. UNA-Australia, UNA-Canada, UNA-New Zealand, UNA-South Africa, UNA-UK, etc.), as well as the global union of national associations, the World Federation of United Nations Associations (WFUNA).

Most United Nations Associations have youth programmes and wings either within their scope of work or as separate United Nations Youth Associations (UNYA). You can find out more about how youth can get involved by contacting your local UNA directly.

For more information, visit the site of the World Federation of United Nations Associations: *www.wfuna.org*.

National offices of United Nations agencies

The United Nations Children's Fund (UNICEF) has national committees in many countries that spread awareness about UNICEF's programmes and raise funds to help them become a reality.

Some 3,600 United Nations Educational, Scientific and Cultural Organization (UNESCO) clubs, centres and associations (all affiliated with UNESCO) in over 90 countries undertake activities in the areas of education, science, culture and communication.

United Nations Information Centres (UNICS)

The United Nations maintains Information Centres (UNICs) and other major contact points all over the world.

You can find a list of UNICs online at: *http://unic.un.org*

United Nations Volunteers (UNV)

If you have a skill in such fields as agriculture, medicine, education, information technology, vocational training, the promotion of human rights or industry—as well as the necessary flexibility and commitment—the United Nations Volunteers (UNV) programme may be right for you. The programme places volunteers, for a one-to-two-year period, with an appropriate United Nations development project in a developing country.

For more information on the programme, visit *www.unv.org*

Campaigns and social media

You can get involved in specific campaigns advertised throughout the United Nations and those of other organizations in the United Nations family. These campaigns aim to feed hungry people, stop rape in conflict, eliminate violence against women, end child labour and more.

You can also participate in the conversation on social media such as Facebook and Twitter. The UN family has a significant presence in social media, one example being *www.facebook.com/unpublications.*

How can young people get to know and experience the United Nations?

Young people are a top priority for the United Nations, as they represent a new generation of support. Several hundred Model United Nations conferences are organized every year at all educational levels, from primary school to university, in many different configurations and countries. Many of today's leaders in law, government, business and the arts participated in Model United Nations programmes during their childhood.

At the Global Model United Nations (GMUN) Conference, students from every region of the world role-play as foreign diplomats and participate in simulated sessions of the United Nations General Assembly and other multilateral bodies in the United Nations system. While preparing for a Model United Nations conference, students develop leadership, research, writing, public speaking and problem-solving skills that they will use throughout their lives. In addition, participation encourages consensus building, conflict resolution and cooperation.

Global Model United Nations offers two unique innovations:

- It uses Rules of Procedure that more closely represent how the United Nations functions.

- It provides unparalleled access to United Nations officials and diplomats prior to and during the conference.

Each delegation representing a Member State is made up of students from different countries.

Can the United Nations provide me with financial assistance?

The United Nations does not provide financial assistance to students and has no general scholarship or student exchange programme.

Does the United Nations accept student interns?

The United Nations provides opportunities for students enrolled in a graduate programme to undertake an internship at its Headquarters in New York and at other major locations of the Organization. You can find more information on the internship programme at *www.un.org/depts/ OHRM/sds/internsh/index.htm* or *http://social.un.org/index/Youth/UNOpportunities/ Internships.aspx*.

Working at the United Nations

The United Nations Secretariat is looking for competent and motivated individuals with a strong belief in the Organization's purpose and mandates, who are willing to dedicate themselves to a rewarding international career in different locations around the world. The United Nations provides an opportunity to serve in a dynamic, multicultural environment in a variety of jobs in the support of global causes.

If you are exploring the possibility of a career with the United Nations, browse the job openings and apply. All job openings in the United Nations Secretariat are published on the United Nations Careers Portal, careers.un.org (also available in French). There, you can create your profile, review available listings and submit your application online.

Candidates for jobs in the General Service and related categories, including those in the trades and crafts, security and safety, secretarial and other support positions, are recruited locally.

Competitive Examinations

The United Nations offers the Young Professionals Programme for Junior Professionals, a recruitment initiative that brings new talent to the Organization through an annual entrance examination. The United Nations also holds examinations for positions requiring special language skills. Information on both types of competitive examinations is available online at *careers.un.org*

Associate Experts Programme

This programme offers young professionals who are graduates from universities or institutions of higher education an opportunity to work on development or regional projects and acquire professional experience in their fields with the technical cooperation of the United Nations Secretariat.

More information on the programme can be found at *http://esa.un.org/tech-coop/ associateexperts/index.html*.

Job Opportunities in the United Nations System

If you are interested in working for other United Nations agencies, funds or programmes, please visit their websites directly. Most websites can be accessed through the links found at the International Civil Service Commission: *http://icsc.un.org/secretariat/includes/joblinks.asp.*

Warning to Applicants

There are job advertisements and offers that falsely state that they are from the United Nations. Please be aware that the United Nations does not request payment at any stage of the application and review process.

Where can I get information about a United Nations Member State's position on various current issues?

You can obtain such information from the Permanent Mission to the United Nations of the country concerned. The list of contact information and websites for the Member States can be found at *www.un.org/en/members.*

UNITED NATIONS OBSERVANCES

United Nations observances contribute to the achievement of the purposes of the United Nations Charter and promote awareness of and action on important political, social, cultural, humanitarian or human rights issues. They provide a useful means for the promotion of international and national action and stimulate interest in United Nations activities and programmes.

For more information, visit *www.un.org/en/events/observances/index.shtml.*

International Decades

2016–2025	United Nations Decade of Action on Nutrition
2015–2024	International Decade for People of African Descent
2014–2024	United Nations Decade of Sustainable Energy for All
2011–2020	Third International Decade for the Eradication of Colonialism
	United Nations Decade on Biodiversity
	Decade of Action for Road Safety
2010–2020	United Nations Decade for Deserts and the Fight against Desertification
2008–2017	Second United Nations Decade for the Eradication of Poverty
2006–2016	Decade of Recovery and Sustainable Development of the Affected Regions (third decade after the Chernobyl disaster)

International Years

2017	International Year of Sustainable Tourism for Development
2016	International Year of Pulses
2015	International Year of Light and Light-based Technologies
	International Year of Soils (FAO)
2014	International Year of Solidarity with the Palestinian People

Annual Weeks

First week of February	World Interfaith Harmony Week
21–27 March	Week of Solidarity with the Peoples Struggling against Racism and Racial Discrimination
19–23 April	Global Soil Week
24–30 April	World Immunization Week (WHO)
25–31 May	Week of Solidarity with the Peoples of Non-Self-Governing Territories
1–7 August	World Breastfeeding Week (WHO)
4–10 October	World Space Week
24–30 October	Disarmament Week
The week of 11 November	International Week of Science and Peace

Annual Days

27 January	International Day of Commemoration in Memory of the Victims of the Holocaust
4 February	World Cancer Day (WHO)
6 February	International Day of Zero Tolerance to Female Genital Mutilation (WHO)
11 February	International Day of Women and Girls in Science
13 February	World Radio Day (UNESCO)
20 February	World Day of Social Justice
21 February	International Mother Language Day (UNESCO)
1 March	Zero Discrimination Day (UNAIDS)
3 March	World Wildlife Day
8 March	International Women's Day
20 March	International Day of Happiness
	French Language Day
21 March	International Day for the Elimination of Racial Discrimination
	World Poetry Day
	International Day of Nowruz
	World Down Syndrome Day
	International Day of Forests
22 March	World Water Day
23 March	World Meteorological Day (WMO)
24 March	International Day for the Right to the Truth concerning Gross Human Rights Violations and for the Dignity of Victims
	World Tuberculosis Day (WHO)
25 March	International Day of Remembrance of the Victims of Slavery and the Transatlantic Slave Trade
	International Day of Solidarity with Detained and Missing Staff Members
2 April	World Autism Awareness Day
4 April	International Day for Mine Awareness and Assistance in Mine Action
6 April	International Day of Sport for Development and Peace
7 April	World Health Day (WHO)
	International Day of Reflection on the Genocide in Rwanda
12 April	International Day of Human Space Flight
20 April	Chinese Language Day
22 April	International Mother Earth Day
23 April	World Book and Copyright Day (UNESCO)
	English Language Day
	Spanish Language Day
25 April	World Malaria Day (WHO)
26 April	International Chernobyl Disaster Remembrance Day
	World Intellectual Property Day (WIPO)
28 April	World Day for Safety and Health at Work (ILO)

29 April	Day of Remembrance for all Victims of Chemical Warfare
30 April	International Jazz Day (UNESCO)
3 May	World Tuna Day
	World Press Freedom Day
8–9 May	Time of Remembrance and Reconciliation for Those Who Lost Their Lives during the Second World War
10 May	World Migratory Bird Day (UNEP)
	"Vesak", the Day of the Full Moon
15 May	International Day of Families
17 May	World Telecommunication and Information Society Day (ITU)
21 May	World Day for Cultural Diversity for Dialogue and Development
22 May	International Day for Biological Diversity
23 May	International Day to End Obstetric Fistula
29 May	International Day of UN Peacekeepers
31 May	World No-Tobacco Day (WHO)
1 June	Global Day of Parents
4 June	International Day of Innocent Children Victims of Aggression
5 June	World Environment Day (UNEP)
6 June	Russian Language Day
8 June	World Oceans Day
12 June	World Day Against Child Labour (ILO)
13 June	International Albinism Awareness Day
14 June	World Blood Donor Day (WHO)
15 June	World Elder Abuse Awareness Day
16 June	International Day of Family Remittances
17 June	World Day to Combat Desertification and Drought
19 June	International Day for the Elimination of Sexual Violence in Conflict
20 June	World Refugee Day
21 June	International Day of Yoga
23 June	International Widows' Day
	United Nations Public Service Day
25 June	Day of the Seafarer (IMO)
26 June	International Day against Drug Abuse and Illicit Trafficking
	United Nations International Day in Support of Victims of Torture
30 June	International Asteroid Day
First Saturday of July	International Day of Cooperatives
11 July	World Population Day
15 July	World Youth Skills Day
18 July	Nelson Mandela International Day
28 July	World Hepatitis Day (WHO)
30 July	International Day of Friendship
	World Day against Trafficking in Persons
9 August	International Day of the World's Indigenous People
12 August	International Youth Day
19 August	World Humanitarian Day

23 August	International Day for the Remembrance of the Slave Trade and Its Abolition (UNESCO)
29 August	International Day against Nuclear Tests
30 August	International Day of the Victims of Enforced Disappearances
5 September	International Day of Charity
8 September	International Literacy Day (UNESCO)
12 September	United Nations Day for South-South Cooperation
15 September	International Day of Democracy
16 September	International Day for the Preservation of the Ozone Layer
21 September	International Day of Peace
26 September	International Day for the Total Elimination of Nuclear Weapons
27 September	World Tourism Day (UNWTO)
28 September	World Rabies Day (WHO)
Last Thursday of September	World Maritime Day (IMO)
1 October	International Day of Older Persons
2 October	International Day of Non-Violence
First Monday in October	World Habitat Day
5 October	World Teachers' Day (UNESCO)
9 October	World Post Day (UPU)
10 October	World Mental Health Day (WHO)
11 October	International Day of the Girl Child
13 October	International Day for Disaster Reduction
15 October	International Day of Rural Women
16 October	World Food Day (FAO)
17 October	International Day for the Eradication of Poverty
20 October (every 5 years, beginning in 2010)	World Statistics Day
24 October	United Nations Day
	World Development Information Day
27 October	World Day for Audiovisual Heritage (UNESCO)
31 October	World Cities Day
2 November	International Day to End Impunity for Crimes against Journalists
5 November	World Tsunami Awareness Day
6 November	International Day for Preventing the Exploitation of the Environment in War and Armed Conflict
10 November	World Science Day for Peace and Development (UNESCO)
14 November	World Diabetes Day (WHO)
16 November	International Day for Tolerance
Third Thursday in November	World Philosophy Day (UNESCO)
Third Sunday in November	World Day of Remembrance for Road Traffic Victims (WHO)
19 November	World Toilet Day
20 November	Africa Industrialization Day
	Universal Children's Day
21 November	World Television Day
25 November	International Day for the Elimination of Violence against Women

29 November	International Day of Solidarity with the Palestinian People
1 December	World AIDS Day
2 December	International Day for the Abolition of Slavery
3 December	International Day of Persons with Disabilities
5 December	World Soil Day
	International Volunteer Day for Economic and Social Development
7 December	International Civil Aviation Day (ICAO)
9 December	International Anti-Corruption Day
	International Day of Commemoration and Dignity of the Victims of the Crime of Genocide and of the Prevention of this Crime
10 December	Human Rights Day
11 December	International Mountain Day
18 December	International Migrants Day
	Arabic Language Day
20 December	International Human Solidarity Day

The United Nations System

UN PRINCIPAL ORGANS

GENERAL ASSEMBLY

SECURITY COUNCIL

ECONOMIC AND SOCIAL COUNCIL

SECRETARIAT

INTERNATIONAL COURT OF JUSTICE

TRUSTEESHIP COUNCIL[6]

Subsidiary Organs

- Main Committees
- Disarmament Commission
- Human Rights Council
- International Law Commission
- Joint Inspection Unit (JIU)
- Standing committees and ad hoc bodies

Funds and Programmes[1]

UNDP United Nations Development Programme
- **UNCDF** United Nations Capital Development Fund
- **UNV** United Nations Volunteers

UNEP[8] United Nations Environment Programme

UNFPA United Nations Population Fund

UN-Habitat[8] United Nations Human Settlements Programme

UNICEF United Nations Children's Fund

WFP World Food Programme (UN/FAO)

Subsidiary Organs

- Counter-Terrorism Committee
- International Tribunal for the former Yugoslavia (ICTY)
- International Residual Mechanism for Criminal Tribunals
- Military Staff Committee

Functional Commissions

- Crime Prevention and Criminal Justice
- Narcotic Drugs
- Population and Development
- Science and Technology for Development
- Social Development
- Statistics
- Status of Women
- United Nations Forum on Forests

Regional Commissions

ECA Economic Commission for Afric

ECE Economic Commission for Europ

ECLAC Economic Commission for Latin America and the Caribbean

ESCAP Economic and Social Commission for Asia and the Pacit

ESCWA Economic and Social Commission for Western Asia

Departments and Offices[9]

EOSG Executive Office of the Secretary-General

DESA Department of Economic and Social Affairs

DFS Department of Field Support

DGACM Department for General Assembly and Conference Management

DM Department of Management

DPA Department of Political Affairs

DPI Department of Public Information

DPKO Department of Peacekeeping Operations

DSS Department of Safety and Security

OCHA Office for the Coordination of Humanitarian Affairs

ODA Office for Disarmament Affairs

OHCHR Office of the United Nations High Commissioner for Human Rights

OIOS Office of Internal Oversight Services

OLA Office of Legal Affairs

OSAA Office of the Special Adviser on Africa

PBSO Peacebuilding Support Office

SRSG/CAAC Office of the Special Representative of the Secretary-General for Children and Armed Conflict

SRSG/SVC Office of the Special Representative of the Secretary-General on Sexual Violence in Conflict

SRSG/VAC Office of the Special Representative of the Secretary-General on Violence Against Children

UNISDR United Nations Office for Disaster Risk Reduction

UNODC[1] United Nations Office on Drugs and Crime

Research and Training

UNIDIR United Nations Institute for Disarmament Research

UNITAR United Nations Institute for Training and Research

UNSSC United Nations System Staff College

UNU United Nations University

Other Entities

ITC International Trade Centre (UN/WTO)

UNCTAD[1,8] United Nations Conference on Trade and Development

UNHCR[1] Office of the United Nations High Commissioner for Refugees

UNOPS[1] United Nations Office for Project Services

UNRWA[1] United Nations Relief and Works Agency for Palestine Refugees in the Near East

UN-Women[1] United Nations Entity for Gender Equality and the Empowerment of Women

Related Organizations

CTBTO Preparatory Commission Preparatory Commission for the Comprehensive Nuclear-Test-Ban Treaty Organization

IAEA[1,3] International Atomic Energy Agency

ICC International Criminal Court

IOM[1] International Organization for Migration

ISA International Seabed Authority

ITLOS International Tribunal for the Law of the Sea

OPCW[3] Organization for the Prohibition of Chemical Weapons

WTO[1,4] World Trade Organization

 Peacebuilding Commission

 HLPF High-level political forum on sustainable development

- Peacekeeping operations and political missions
- Sanctions committees (ad hoc)
- Standing committees and ad hoc bodies

Other Bodies

- Committee for Development Policy
- Committee of Experts on Public Administration
- Committee on Non-Governmental Organizations
- Permanent Forum on Indigenous Issues

UNAIDS Joint United Nations Programme on HIV/AIDS

UNGEGN United Nations Group of Experts on Geographical Names

Research and Training

UNICRI United Nations Interregional Crime and Justice Research Institute

UNRISD United Nations Research Institute for Social Development

Specialized Agencies[1,5]

FAO Food and Agriculture Organization of the United Nations

ICAO International Civil Aviation Organization

IFAD International Fund for Agricultural Development

ILO International Labour Organization

IMF International Monetary Fund

IMO International Maritime Organization

ITU International Telecommunication Union

UNESCO United Nations Educational, Scientific and Cultural Organization

UNIDO United Nations Industrial Development Organization

UNWTO World Tourism Organization

UPU Universal Postal Union

WHO World Health Organization

WIPO World Intellectual Property Organization

WMO World Meteorological Organization

WORLD BANK GROUP[7]

- **IBRD** International Bank for Reconstruction and Development
- **IDA** International Development Association
- **IFC** International Finance Corporation

UNOG United Nations Office at Geneva

UN-OHRLLS Office of the High Representative for the Least Developed Countries, Landlocked Developing Countries and Small Island Developing States

UNON United Nations Office at Nairobi

UNOP[2] United Nations Office for Partnerships

UNOV United Nations Office at Vienna

Notes:

1 Members of the United Nations System Chief Executives Board for Coordination (CEB).
2 UN Office for Partnerships (UNOP) is the UN's focal point vis-a-vis the United Nations Foundation, Inc.
3 IAEA and OPCW report to the Security Council and the General Assembly (GA).
4 WTO has no reporting obligation to the GA, but contributes on an ad hoc basis to GA and Economic and Social Council (ECOSOC) work on, inter alia, finance and development issues.
5 Specialized agencies are autonomous organizations whose work is coordinated through ECOSOC (intergovernmental level) and CEB (inter-secretariat level).
6 The Trusteeship Council suspended operation on 1 November 1994, as on 1 October 1994 Palau, the last United Nations Trust Territory, became independent.
7 International Centre for Settlement of Investment Disputes (ICSID) and Multilateral Investment Guarantee Agency (MIGA) are not specialized agencies in accordance with Articles 57 and 63 of the Charter, but are part of the World Bank Group.
8 The secretariats of these organs are part of the UN Secretariat.
9 The Secretariat also includes the following offices: The Ethics Office, United Nations Ombudsman and Mediation Services, Office of Administration of Justice and the Office on Sport for Development and Peace

This Chart is a reflection of the functional organization of the United Nations System and for informational purposes only. It does not include all offices or entities of the United Nations System.

Published by the United Nations Department of Public Information DPI/2470 rev.5 —17-00023—March 2017

MEMBER STATES

Membership in the United Nations has grown from 51 States in 1945 to 193 in 2018. States are admitted by decision of the General Assembly upon recommendation of the Security Council.

Member State	Population (est.) For 2017	Date of admission
Afghanistan	29,117,000	19 November 1946
Albania	3,169,000	14 December 1955
Algeria	35,423,000	8 October 1962
Andorra	87,000	28 July 1993
Angola	18,993,000	1 December 1976
Antigua and Barbuda	89,000	11 November 1981
Argentina	40,666,000	24 October 1945
Armenia	3,090,000	2 March 1992
Australia	21,512,000	1 November 1945
Austria	8,387,000	14 December 1955
Azerbaijan	8,934,000	2 March 1992
Bahamas	346,000	18 September 1973
Bahrain	807,000	21 September 1971
Bangladesh	164,425,000	17 September 1974
Barbados	257,000	9 December 1966
Belarus	9,588,000	24 October 1945
Belgium	10,698,000	27 December 1945
Belize	313,000	25 September 1981
Benin	9,212,000	20 September 1960
Bhutan	708,000	21 September 1971
Bolivia (Plurinational State of)	10,031,000	14 November 1945
Bosnia and Herzegovina	3,760,000	22 May 1992
Botswana	1,978,000	17 October 1966
Brazil	195,423,000	24 October 1945
Brunei Darussalam	407,000	21 September 1984
Bulgaria	7,497,000	14 December 1955
Burkina Faso	16,287,000	20 September 1960
Burundi	8,519,000	18 September 1962
Cambodia	15,053,000	14 December 1955
Cameroon	19,958,000	20 September 1960
Canada	33,890,000	9 November 1945
Cape Verde	513,000	16 September 1975
Central African Republic	4,506,000	20 September 1960
Chad	11,506,000	20 September 1960
Chile	17,135,000	24 October 1945
China	1,354,146,000	24 October 1945
Colombia	46,300,000	5 November 1945

Member State	Population (est.) For 2017	Date of admission
Comoros	691,000	12 November 1975
Congo	3,759,000	20 September 1960
Costa Rica	4,640,000	2 November 1945
Côte d'Ivoire	21,571,000	20 September 1960
Croatia	4,410,000	22 May 1992
Cuba	11,204,000	24 October 1945
Cyprus	880,000	20 September 1960
Czech Republic	10,411,000	19 January 1993
Democratic People's Republic of Korea	23,991,000	17 September 1991
Democratic Republic of the Congo	67,827,000	20 September 1960
Denmark	5,481,000	24 October 1945
Djibouti	879,000	20 September 1977
Dominica	67,000	18 December 1978
Dominican Republic	10,225,000	24 October 1945
Ecuador	13,775,000	21 December 1945
Egypt	84,474,000	24 October 1945
El Salvador	6,194,000	24 October 1945
Equatorial Guinea	693,000	12 November 1968
Eritrea	5,224,000	28 May 1993
Estonia	1,339,000	17 September 1991
Ethiopia	84,976,000	13 November 1945
Fiji	854,000	13 October 1970
Finland	5,346,000	14 December 1955
France	62,637,000	24 October 1945
Gabon	1,501,000	20 September 1960
Gambia	1,751,000	21 September 1965
Georgia	4,219,000	31 July 1992
Germany	82,057,000	18 September 1973
Ghana	24,333,000	8 March 1957
Greece	11,183,000	25 October 1945
Grenada	104,000	17 September 1974
Guatemala	14,377,000	21 November 1945
Guinea	10,324,000	12 December 1958
Guinea-Bissau	1,647,000	17 September 1974
Guyana	761,000	20 September 1966
Haiti	10,188,000	24 October 1945
Honduras	7,616,000	17 December 1945
Hungary	9,973,000	14 December 1955
Iceland	329,000	19 November 1946
India	1,214,464,000	30 October 1945
Indonesia	232,517,000	28 September 1950
Iran (Islamic Republic of)	75,078,000	24 October 1945
Iraq	31,467,000	21 December 1945

Member State	Population (est.) For 2017	Date of admission
Ireland	4,589,000	14 December 1955
Israel	7,285,000	11 May 1949
Italy	60,098,000	14 December 1955
Jamaica	2,730,000	18 September 1962
Japan	126,995,000	18 December 1956
Jordan	6,472,000	14 December 1955
Kazakhstan	15,753,000	2 March 1992
Kenya	40,863,000	16 December 1963
Kiribati	100,000	14 September 1999
Kuwait	3,051,000	14 May 1963
Kyrgyzstan	5,550,000	2 March 1992
Lao People's Democratic Republic	6,436,000	14 December 1955
Latvia	2,240,000	17 September 1991
Lebanon	4,255,000	24 October 1945
Lesotho	2,084,000	17 October 1966
Liberia	4,102,000	2 November 1945
Libya	6,546,000	14 December 1955
Liechtenstein	36,000	18 September 1990
Lithuania	3,255,000	17 September 1991
Luxembourg	492,000	24 October 1945
Madagascar	20,146,000	20 September 1960
Malawi	15,692,000	1 December 1964
Malaysia	27,914,000	17 September 1957
Maldives	314,000	21 September 1965
Mali	13,323,000	28 September 1960
Malta	410,000	1 December 1964
Marshall Islands	63,000	17 September 1991
Mauritania	3,366,000	27 October 1961
Mauritius	1,297,000	24 April 1968
Mexico	110,645,000	7 November 1945
Micronesia (Federated States of)	111,000	17 September 1991
Moldova (Republic of)	3,576,000	2 March 1992
Monaco	33,000	28 May 1993
Mongolia	2,701,000	27 October 1961
Montenegro	626,000	28 June 2006
Morocco	32,381,000	12 November 1956
Mozambique	23,406,000	16 September 1975
Myanmar	50,496,000	19 April 1948
Namibia	2,212,000	23 April 1990
Nauru	10,000	14 September 1999
Nepal	29,853,000	14 December 1955
Netherlands	16,653,000	10 December 1945
New Zealand	4,303,000	24 October 1945

Member State	Population (est.) For 2017	Date of admission
Nicaragua	5,822,000	24 October 1945
Niger	15,891,000	20 September 1960
Nigeria	158,259,000	7 October 1960
Norway	4,855,000	27 November 1945
Oman	2,905,000	7 October 1971
Pakistan	184,753,000	30 September 1947
Palau	21,000	15 December 1994
Panama	3,508,000	13 November 1945
Papua New Guinea	6,888,000	10 October 1975
Paraguay	6,460,000	24 October 1945
Peru	29,496,000	31 October 1945
Philippines	93,617,000	24 October 1945
Poland	38,038,000	24 October 1945
Portugal	10,732,000	14 December 1955
Qatar	1,508,000	21 September 1971
Republic of Korea	48,501,000	17 September 1991
Romania	21,190,000	14 December 1955
Russian Federation	140,367,000	24 October 1945
Rwanda	10,277,000	18 September 1962
Saint Kitts and Nevis	52,000	23 September 1983
Saint Lucia	174,000	18 September 1979
Saint Vincent and the Grenadines	109,000	16 September 1980
Samoa	179,000	15 December 1976
San Marino	32,000	2 March 1992
Sao Tome and Principe	165,000	16 September 1975
Saudi Arabia	26,246,000	24 October 1945
Senegal	12,861,000	28 September 1960
Serbia	9,856,000	1 November 2000
Seychelles	85,000	21 September 1976
Sierra Leone	5,836,000	27 September 1961
Singapore	4,837,000	21 September 1965
Slovakia	5,412,000	19 January 1993
Slovenia	2,025,000	22 May 1992
Solomon Islands	536,000	19 September 1978
Somalia	9,359,000	20 September 1960
South Africa	50,492,000	7 November 1945
South Sudan	8,260,490	14 July 2011
Spain	45,317,000	14 December 1955
Sri Lanka	20,410,000	14 December 1955
Sudan	43,192,000	12 November 1956
Suriname	524,000	4 December 1975
Swaziland	1,202,000	24 September 1968
Sweden	9,293,000	19 November 1946

Member State	Population (est.) For 2017	Date of admission
Switzerland	7,595,000	10 September 2002
Syrian Arab Republic	22,505,000	24 October 1945
Tajikistan	7,075,000	2 March 1992
Thailand	68,139,000	16 December 1946
The former Yugoslav Republic of Macedonia	2,043,000	8 April 1993
Timor-Leste	1,171,000	27 September 2002
Togo	6,780,000	20 September 1960
Tonga	104,000	14 September 1999
Trinidad and Tobago	1,344,000	18 September 1962
Tunisia	10,374,000	12 November 1956
Turkey	75,705,000	24 October 1945
Turkmenistan	5,177,000	2 March 1992
Tuvalu	10,000	5 September 2000
Uganda	33,796,000	25 October 1962
Ukraine	45,433,000	24 October 1945
United Arab Emirates	4,707,000	9 December 1971
United Kingdom	61,899,000	24 October 1945
United Republic of Tanzania	45,040,000	14 December 1961
United States of America	317,641,000	24 October 1945
Uruguay	3,372,000	18 December 1945
Uzbekistan	27,794,000	2 March 1992
Vanuatu	246,000	15 September 1981
Venezuela (Bolivarian Republic of)	29,044,000	15 November 1945
Viet Nam	89,029,000	20 September 1977
Yemen	24,256,000	30 September 1947
Zambia	13,257,000	1 December 1964
Zimbabwe	12,644,000	25 August 1980

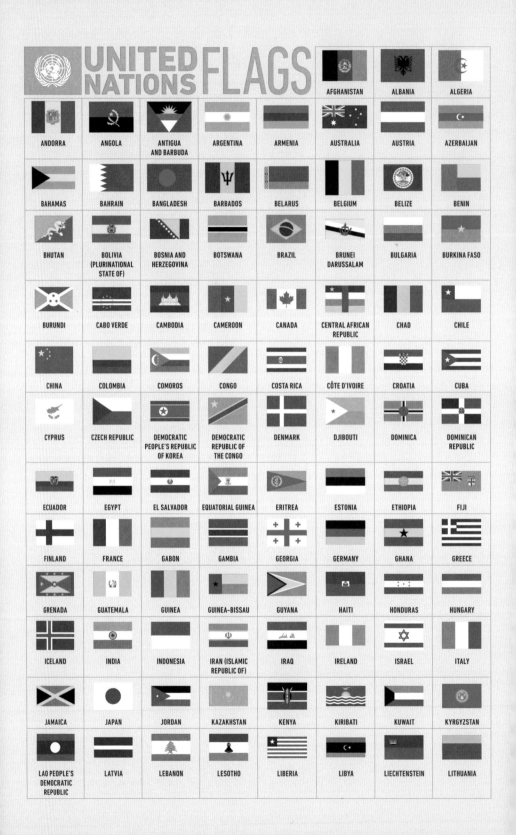

UNITED NATIONS FLAGS

AFGHANISTAN	ALBANIA	ALGERIA

ANDORRA	ANGOLA	ANTIGUA AND BARBUDA	ARGENTINA	ARMENIA	AUSTRALIA	AUSTRIA	AZERBAIJAN
BAHAMAS	BAHRAIN	BANGLADESH	BARBADOS	BELARUS	BELGIUM	BELIZE	BENIN
BHUTAN	BOLIVIA (PLURINATIONAL STATE OF)	BOSNIA AND HERZEGOVINA	BOTSWANA	BRAZIL	BRUNEI DARUSSALAM	BULGARIA	BURKINA FASO
BURUNDI	CABO VERDE	CAMBODIA	CAMEROON	CANADA	CENTRAL AFRICAN REPUBLIC	CHAD	CHILE
CHINA	COLOMBIA	COMOROS	CONGO	COSTA RICA	CÔTE D'IVOIRE	CROATIA	CUBA
CYPRUS	CZECH REPUBLIC	DEMOCRATIC PEOPLE'S REPUBLIC OF KOREA	DEMOCRATIC REPUBLIC OF THE CONGO	DENMARK	DJIBOUTI	DOMINICA	DOMINICAN REPUBLIC
ECUADOR	EGYPT	EL SALVADOR	EQUATORIAL GUINEA	ERITREA	ESTONIA	ETHIOPIA	FIJI
FINLAND	FRANCE	GABON	GAMBIA	GEORGIA	GERMANY	GHANA	GREECE
GRENADA	GUATEMALA	GUINEA	GUINEA-BISSAU	GUYANA	HAITI	HONDURAS	HUNGARY
ICELAND	INDIA	INDONESIA	IRAN (ISLAMIC REPUBLIC OF)	IRAQ	IRELAND	ISRAEL	ITALY
JAMAICA	JAPAN	JORDAN	KAZAKHSTAN	KENYA	KIRIBATI	KUWAIT	KYRGYZSTAN
LAO PEOPLE'S DEMOCRATIC REPUBLIC	LATVIA	LEBANON	LESOTHO	LIBERIA	LIBYA	LIECHTENSTEIN	LITHUANIA

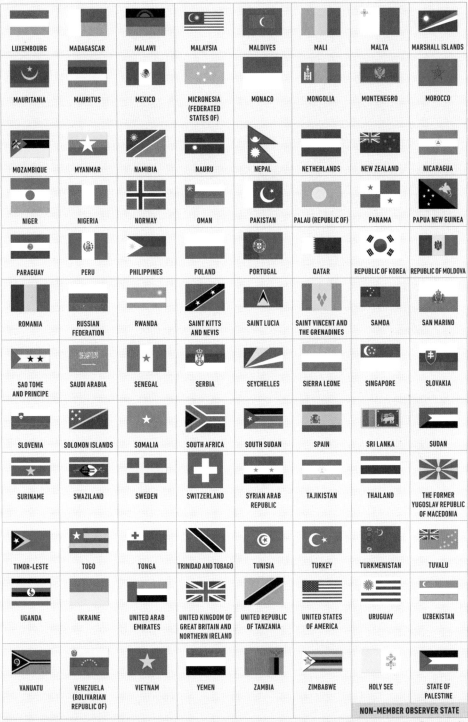

LUXEMBOURG	MADAGASCAR	MALAWI	MALAYSIA	MALDIVES	MALI	MALTA	MARSHALL ISLANDS
MAURITANIA	MAURITIUS	MEXICO	MICRONESIA (FEDERATED STATES OF)	MONACO	MONGOLIA	MONTENEGRO	MOROCCO
MOZAMBIQUE	MYANMAR	NAMIBIA	NAURU	NEPAL	NETHERLANDS	NEW ZEALAND	NICARAGUA
NIGER	NIGERIA	NORWAY	OMAN	PAKISTAN	PALAU (REPUBLIC OF)	PANAMA	PAPUA NEW GUINEA
PARAGUAY	PERU	PHILIPPINES	POLAND	PORTUGAL	QATAR	REPUBLIC OF KOREA	REPUBLIC OF MOLDOVA
ROMANIA	RUSSIAN FEDERATION	RWANDA	SAINT KITTS AND NEVIS	SAINT LUCIA	SAINT VINCENT AND THE GRENADINES	SAMOA	SAN MARINO
SAO TOME AND PRINCIPE	SAUDI ARABIA	SENEGAL	SERBIA	SEYCHELLES	SIERRA LEONE	SINGAPORE	SLOVAKIA
SLOVENIA	SOLOMON ISLANDS	SOMALIA	SOUTH AFRICA	SOUTH SUDAN	SPAIN	SRI LANKA	SUDAN
SURINAME	SWAZILAND	SWEDEN	SWITZERLAND	SYRIAN ARAB REPUBLIC	TAJIKISTAN	THAILAND	THE FORMER YUGOSLAV REPUBLIC OF MACEDONIA
TIMOR-LESTE	TOGO	TONGA	TRINIDAD AND TOBAGO	TUNISIA	TURKEY	TURKMENISTAN	TUVALU
UGANDA	UKRAINE	UNITED ARAB EMIRATES	UNITED KINGDOM OF GREAT BRITAIN AND NORTHERN IRELAND	UNITED REPUBLIC OF TANZANIA	UNITED STATES OF AMERICA	URUGUAY	UZBEKISTAN
VANUATU	VENEZUELA (BOLIVARIAN REPUBLIC OF)	VIETNAM	YEMEN	ZAMBIA	ZIMBABWE	HOLY SEE	STATE OF PALESTINE
							NON-MEMBER OBSERVER STATE

Every effort has been made to ensure that the images and text of this poster are complete and accurate. Due to technical reasons, some colours and designs may not comply exactly with official specifications of the flags. All images current as of December 2017.